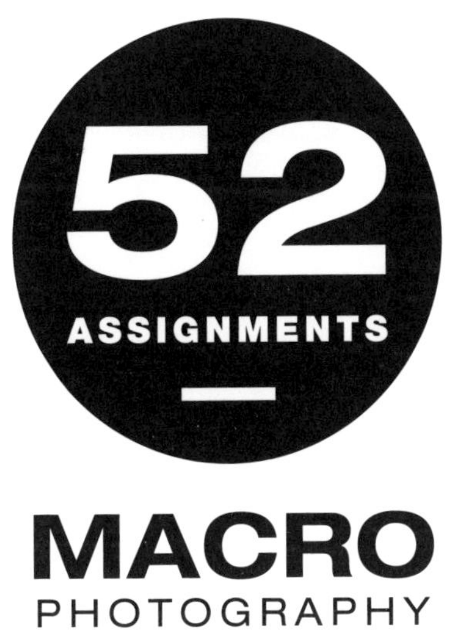

MACRO
PHOTOGRAPHY

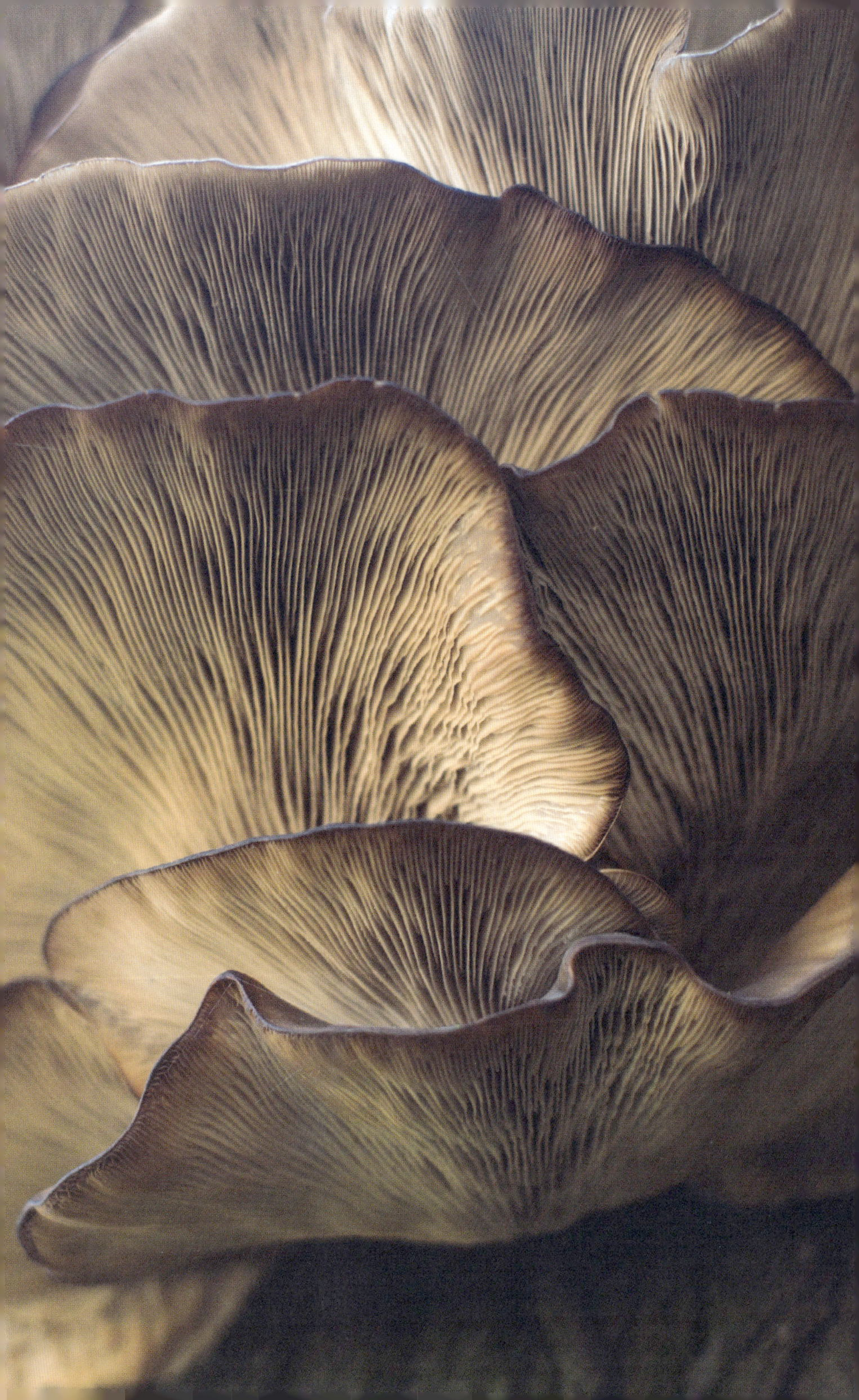

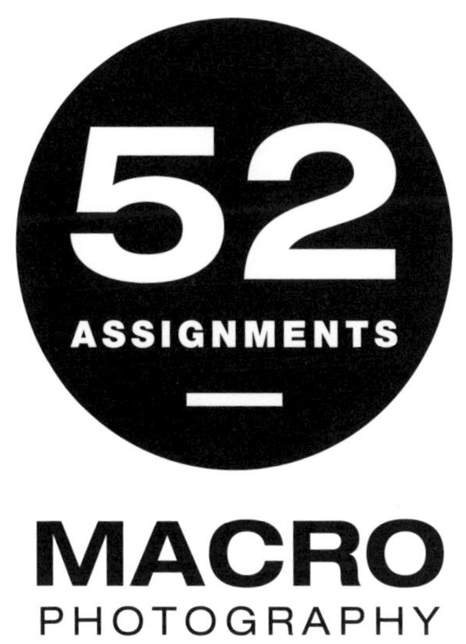

52 ASSIGNMENTS

MACRO
PHOTOGRAPHY

DAVID TAYLOR

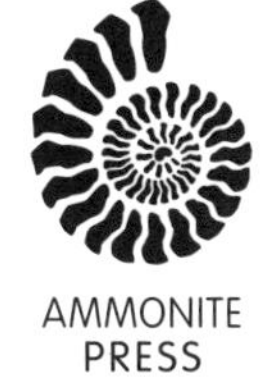

AMMONITE
PRESS

ASSIGNMENTS

Tick off your completed projects

	01	MAGNIFIED	8
	02	CELLPHONE MACRO	10
	03	REVEALING TEXTURE	12
	04	CLOSE-UP FILTERS	14
	05	AT THE BEACH	16
	06	BACK TO FRONT	18
	07	SOFTLY DOES IT	20
	08	TAKING THE TUBE	22
	09	REFLECTED LIGHT	24
	10	FLOWER POWER	26
	11	SILHOUETTE	28
	12	SINGLED OUT	30
	13	ABSTRACTS	32

	14	RAINBOW COLORS	34
	15	MACRO IN MUSEUMS	36
	16	HARD LIGHT	38
	17	BOKEHLICIOUS	40
	18	MAKING A SCENE	42
	19	FROSTY CLOSE-UPS	44
	20	FLAME ON	46
	21	FOSSILS	50
	22	SCANOGRAPHY	54
	23	SLICK TECHNIQUE	56
	24	LIGHT TRAILS	58
	25	IT'S A BUG'S LIFE	60
	26	FROZEN BLOOMS	62

ASSIGNMENT KEY

Each assignment has symbols showing the type of tasks involved.

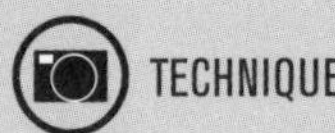

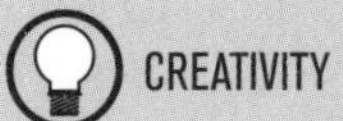

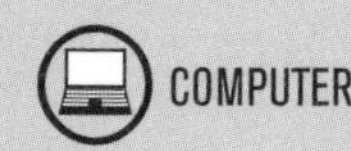

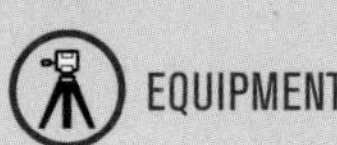

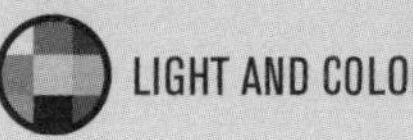

☐	27	HIGH-KEY	64
☐	28	SOFTBOX AND DIFFUSERS	66
☐	29	FUNGI	68
☐	30	JEWELRY	70
☐	31	RINGING AROUND	72
☐	32	COINS AND BANKNOTES	74
☐	33	UP IN SMOKE	76
☐	34	MIXING IT UP	78
☐	35	LOW-KEY	80
☐	36	LIMITING COLOR RANGE	82
☐	37	COMPLETING THE CIRCUIT	84
☐	38	MACRO MOVIES	86
☐	39	PANORAMA	88
☐	40	WARM AND COOL	92
☐	41	THE EYES HAVE IT	94
☐	42	TRANSLUCENCY	96
☐	43	PRODUCT PHOTOGRAPHY	98
☐	44	SOAP BUBBLES	100
☐	45	BLACK AND WHITE	104
☐	46	KITCHEN UTENSILS	106
☐	47	WATER DROPLETS	108
☐	48	INTO THE THIRD DIMENSION	112
☐	49	STACKED	116
☐	50	MUSICAL INSTRUMENTS	120
☐	51	BELLOWS	122
☐	52	SOCIAL MEDIA	124

ASSIGNMENT JOURNAL

Use the journal spaces throughout the book to keep a record of your experimental assignments and images.

INTRODUCTION

Close-up and macro photography helps you see the world in a way that is usually impossible. Look closely at a macro image and you will notice details far too fine for the human eye to resolve.

This book of assignments is a guide to close-up and macro photography. It will push you to try new techniques and experiment more with your photography. There are 52 assignments in total, one for every week in the year. These assignments can be completed in any order, although the more straightforward assignments are near the front of the book and the more complex toward the back. Some of the assignments are also seasonal and so you may need to wait to complete these, or find imaginative alternative subjects.

Macro photography requires equipment with greater capabilities than a camera's standard lens. However, as you'll see in the book, it is possible to shoot close-up and macro images with relatively inexpensive pieces of kit. You certainly don't need to invest in a macro lens to begin working through the assignments. In fact, there's a lot to be said for starting simply and experimenting with close-up photography before you commit to buying a macro lens.

Mastering the art of close-up and macro photography takes time and patience. Progress will not always be smooth and mistakes will be made along the way. However, this is far from unusual as every photographer goes through this process. Learning from your mistakes will make you a better photographer, as will the willingness to push yourself through the occasional failure. Have fun exploring the world of the small—it is a particularly fascinating and rewarding place to spend time in.

David Taylor

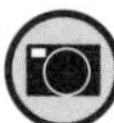

SPECIAL KIT

- Magnifying glass

TIPS

- Use Auto-ISO to maintain a fast shutter speed as you'll only be able to hold your camera with one hand.

- Use a magnifying glass with a wider diameter than the front element of the camera lens.

MAGNIFIED

There are a variety of inexpensive ways to try out macro photography before investing in a macro lens. The simplest method is to hold a magnifying glass in front of a non-macro lens. It sounds odd and makeshift, but it's surprisingly effective.

The results are usually far from perfect, however. Images are rarely pin-sharp, and often suffer from chromatic aberrations and distortions. Molded plastic magnifying glasses are typically worse for this technique than those with a glass lens. The sharpest images are created by holding the magnifying glass parallel to the camera lens. Angling the magnifying glass relative to the lens produces softer and more distorted images, though the results can have an appealing dream-like quality. To focus, you simply move the magnifying glass backward and forward between the lens and the subject until the subject is acceptably sharp.

For this assignment, experiment with a magnifying glass as described above. Use a variety of camera lenses to see which produces the most pleasing images. This technique works well with organic subjects—such as flowers—that don't necessarily require perfect sharpness.

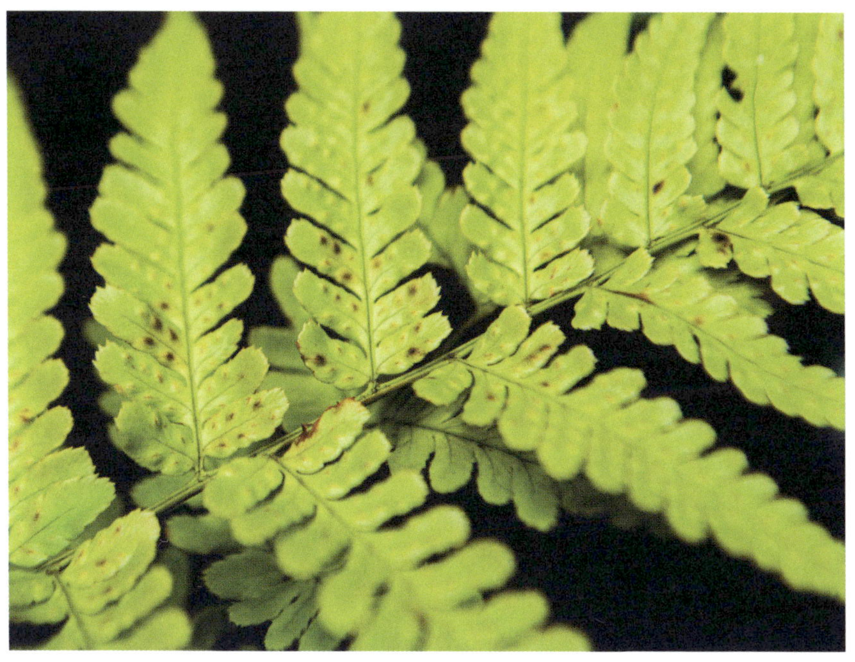

▲ *The sharpest area of a magnifying glass is at its center.*

ASSIGNMENT JOURNAL

MACRO NOTES

Shooting a true 1:1 (life-size) macro image reduces the amount of light hitting the camera's sensor—the greater the magnification, the greater the light loss. The practical effect of this is that shooting a macro image requires using either a longer shutter speed, a wider aperture, or a higher ISO rating. Using a magnifying glass does not create a life-size macro image and so the exposure will be unaffected.

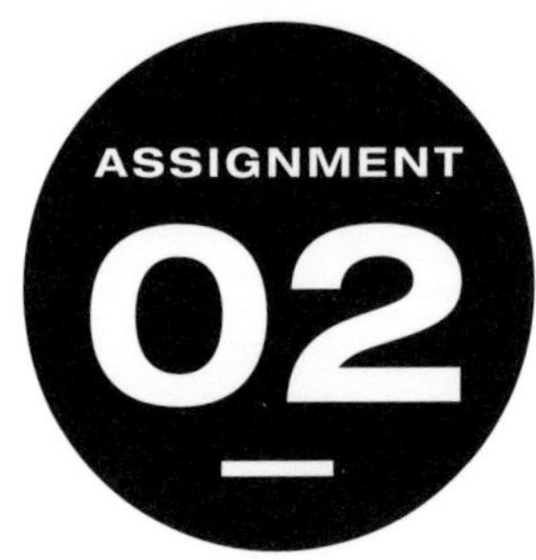

SPECIAL KIT

- Cellphone
- Additional close-up or macro lens
- Image editing app

TIPS

- Hold the phone using all four corners to keep it steady and minimize the risk of shake.
- Before adding the additional lens, remove your camera from any protective case you may have fitted (unless the lens requires a dedicated case).

CELLPHONE MACRO

The cameras on cellphones are capable of producing very pleasing and professional-looking images. Most cellphones can focus at reasonably close distances but are not able to shoot true macro images. However, additional lenses that can add a macro capability are readily available and are relatively inexpensive. These typically clip to the main lens of the phone's camera, or via a dedicated phone case, making them easy to fit and then take off again.

Shooting macro with a cellphone is fun but there are compromises. The working distance will be incredibly small (see assignment 31) leaving very little room between the subject and the phone. Image quality won't be great either, with vivid color fringing often very visible, and distortion will be readily apparent too. However, these problems can be reduced through the use of image editing apps downloaded to your phone. With these you can either correct these problems or alter the style of the image so that they are no longer noticeable. Converting the images to black and white is one option, for example.

Use your cellphone to shoot a series of close-up images, using an additional lens if possible. Think about what type of subject works best using your phone and experiment with lighting to see what results give the best-looking images.

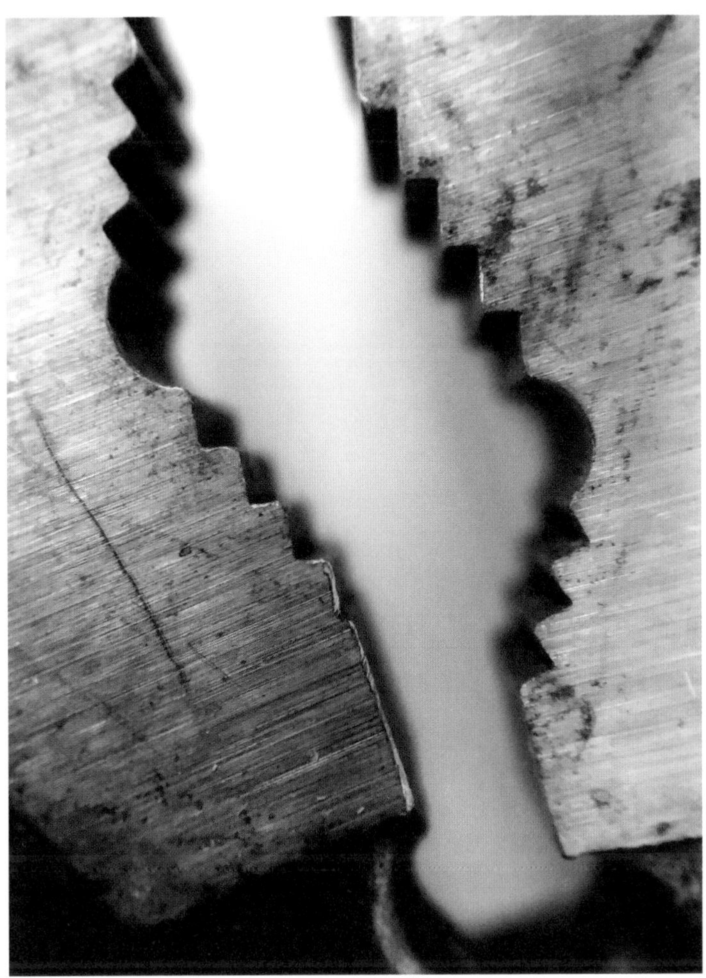

▲ *An app was used here to turn this image to black and white and an atmospheric grain effect was added.*

MACRO NOTES

Cellphones typically don't have a large dynamic range, which is a measure of how much detail a camera can record in both the shadow and the highlight areas. Cellphones often clip highlights in particular, so that no detail is visible at all. HDR, or High Dynamic Range, is a mode often found on phones that can help overcome this problem.

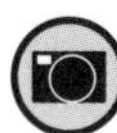

SPECIAL KIT

- Tripod

TIPS

- Shoot with the camera parallel to the surface of your chosen subjects.

- Use an aperture small enough to ensure everything is sharp across the image space.

REVEALING TEXTURE

Every surface has a texture, whether that's smooth or rough, soft or hard, reflective or dull. Macro photography is ideally suited to making texture the sole subject of an image. Shoot sufficiently close to the surface of an object and the photo is likely to reveal only its texture. Shooting textures is a great way to hone your photographic eye. It forces you to look for patterns and to appreciate qualities such as color and shape.

Light plays a big part in the success of texture photography. Side lighting helps to reveal the three-dimensional quality of texture by creating highlights and shadows. How you compose your shots will also be important. Using a tripod will slow you down and make you consider what should and—perhaps more importantly—should not be included in the photo.

Your assignment is to create a short series of photos. Vary the photos by looking for different textures, colors, and patterns. Try shooting in different types of light to see what difference this makes to the look of the photos.

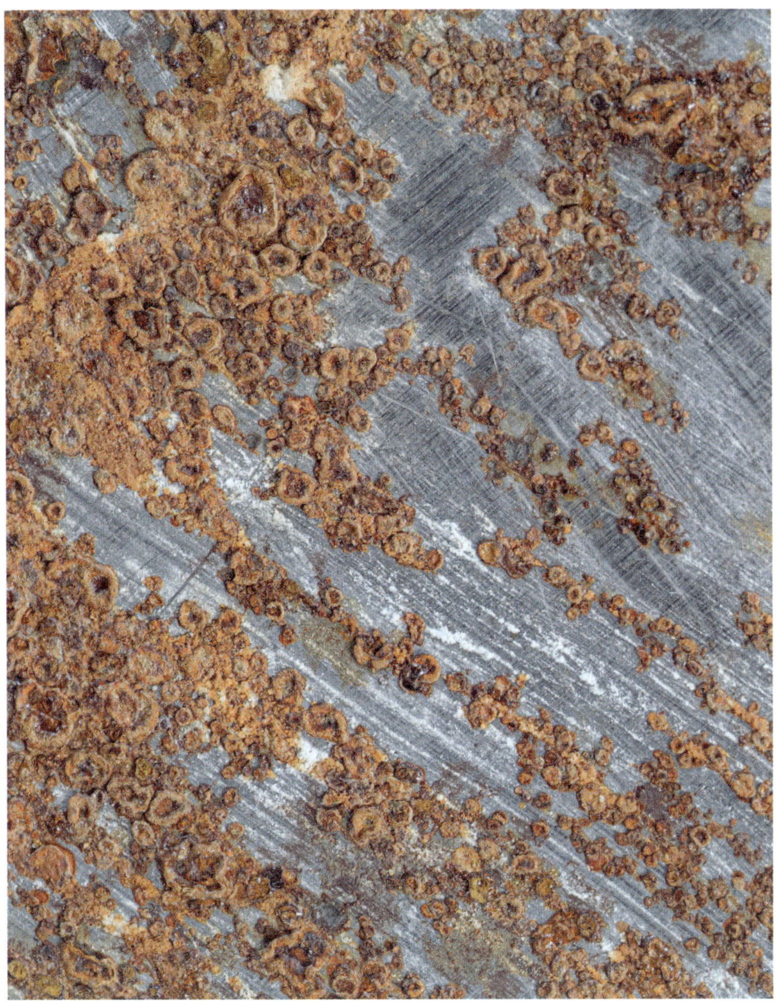

▲ *Rusty metal offers an intriguing mix of different textures and colors.*

MACRO NOTES

Side lighting is created by a light source placed roughly 90° to the camera. The position of the sun changes constantly through the day so how objects outside are lit will also change. Artificial lighting, such as off-camera flash, LED light, or a desk lamp, produces more consistent lighting if you plan to spend time on one particular subject.

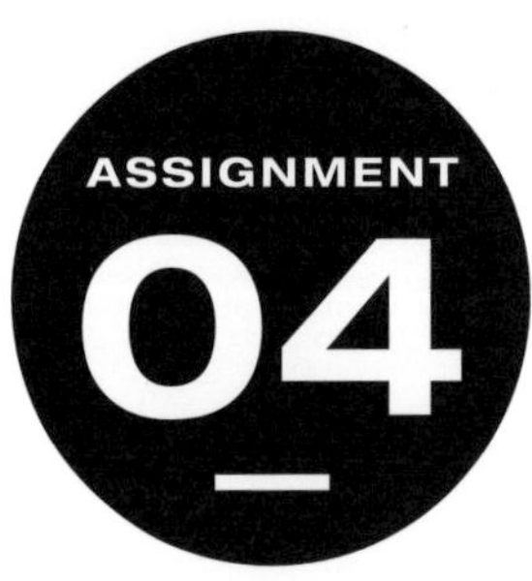

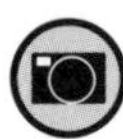

SPECIAL KIT

- Close-up filters

TIPS

- Shoot using a mid-range aperture setting such as f/8 or f/11 to maximize image quality.

- Buy close-up filters to fit the largest filter size of the lenses you own. A step-up ring could then be used to adapt the close-up filters to fit the smaller filter threads of any other lenses you may own.

CLOSE-UP FILTERS

A close-up filter is a simple optic that screws directly onto the filter thread of a lens. As the name suggests, a close-up filter allows the camera lens to focus more closely. Close-up filters are a very inexpensive way to try macro photography. They can also be used with cameras that don't have interchangeable lenses, such as compacts and bridge cameras.

Close-up filters are sold in a variety of different strengths shown as a diopter value; the higher the diopter value, the closer you'll be able to focus and the higher the magnification factor. A diopter of +1 provides modest magnification, whereas a +12 diopter lens will provide 1x magnification on lenses longer than 70mm in focal length. Close-up filters can be stacked to increase magnification, though usually at the expense of image quality.

Your brief for this assignment is to use close-up filters to shoot a macro image. Experiment with how they work and the type of magnification you can achieve. Use a range of different focal lengths, if possible, to see the difference that this makes.

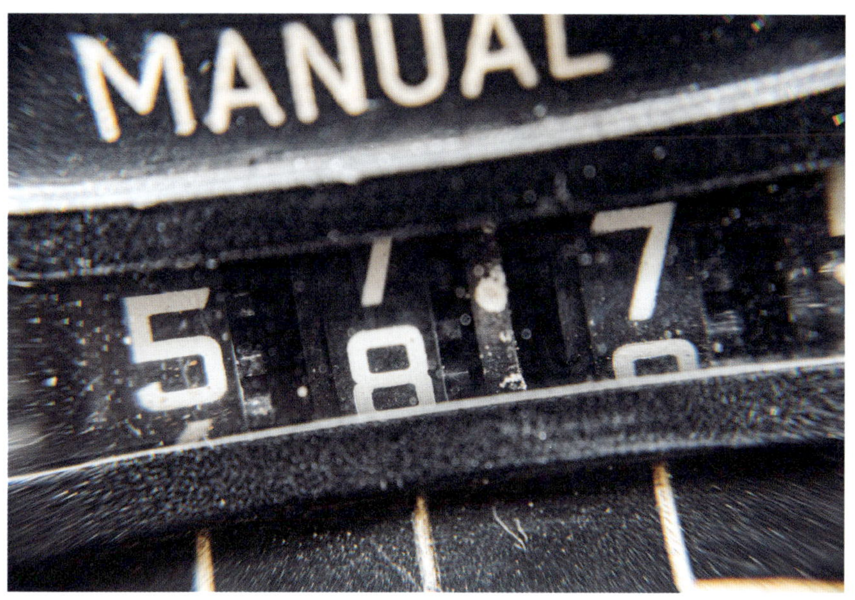

▲ *The very cheapest close-up filters tend to distort the edges of an image and introduce color aberrations.*

ASSIGNMENT JOURNAL

MACRO NOTES

Step-up and step-down rings let you fit a filter or other lens accessory to a lens with a different filter thread size. Step-up rings are used to fit a larger filter or accessory to a smaller filter thread. Step-down rings do the exact opposite and are used to fit a smaller filter or accessory to a larger lens. The filter thread size of a lens is usually found on the inside of the lens cap.

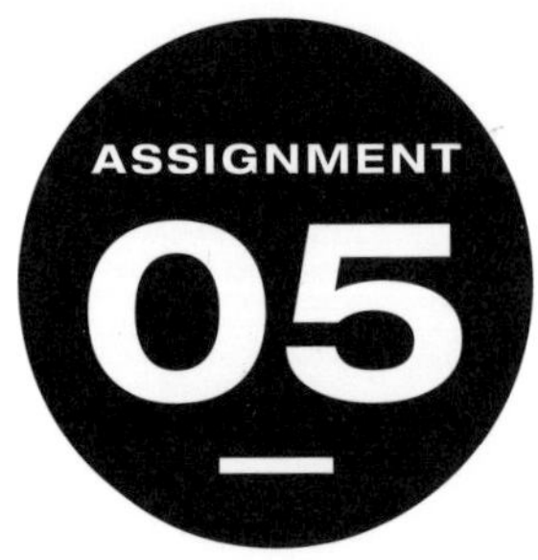

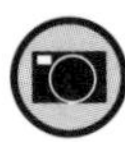

SPECIAL KIT

• Polarizing filter

TIPS

• Shoot early in the morning or late in the afternoon when the sun is lower and the light more interesting.

• River banks and lakes are an alternative to the beach.

• Use a polarizing filter to remove the sheen found on wet rocks and seaweed.

AT THE BEACH

Coastal regions are rewarding places to shoot close-up and macro imagery at any time of year. One challenging aspect of shooting at the coast is the tide, which rises and falls twice daily. Shooting as low tide approaches is the safest option and will allow you to fully explore a beach.

What you can find on a beach will depend on the local geology. Cliffs and rocks are perfect for shooting abstract images, as you can use the patterns made by the cracks and layers in the stone to create interesting results. Shingle, comprised of small pebbles and stones, is often colorful and a jumble of different shapes and textures. Tidal action causes interesting ripples in sand, though foot and paw prints will soon disturb these pristine patterns.

Small mollusks, such as limpets and barnacles, cling to rocks and can also make interesting subjects. Seaweed is commonly found on rocky shorelines too, either as separate specimens or as sheets spread across a large area. The sea also washes in shells and other natural remains, which could be shot in place or arranged in patterns elsewhere on the beach.

Your assignment is to spend a day at the beach and shoot at least ten images. Your selection should be varied and show different aspects of your chosen coastal location.

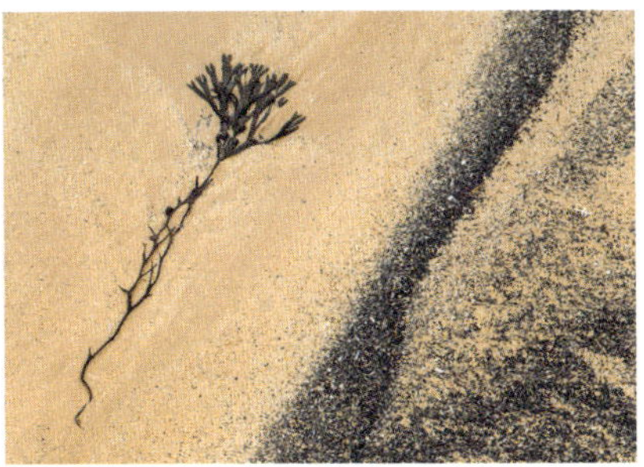
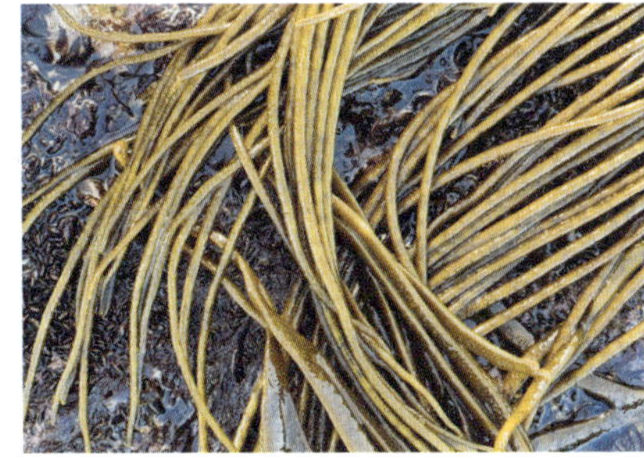
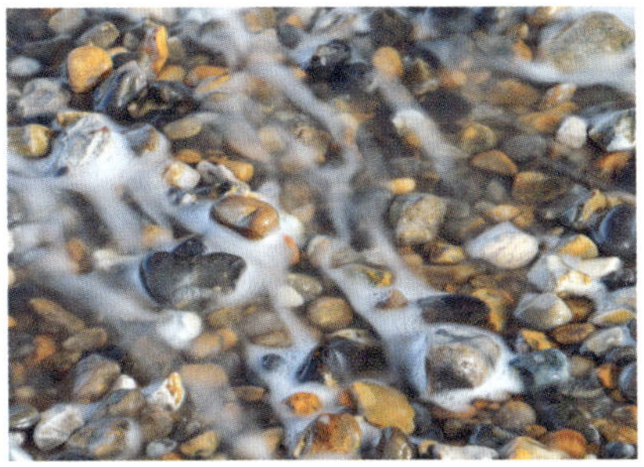
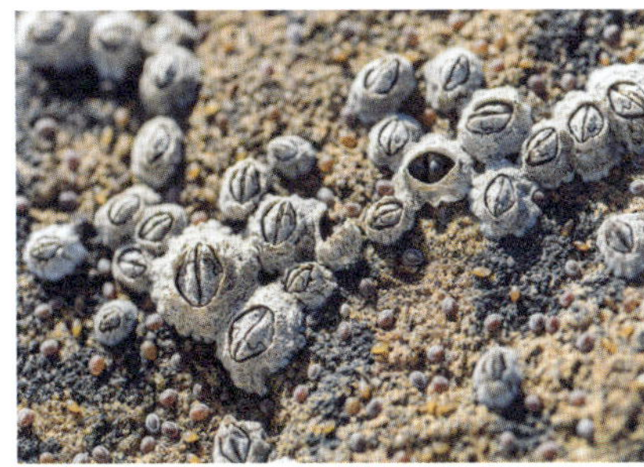
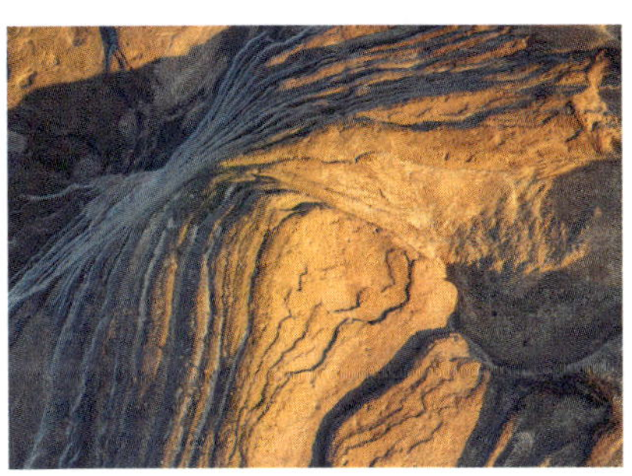
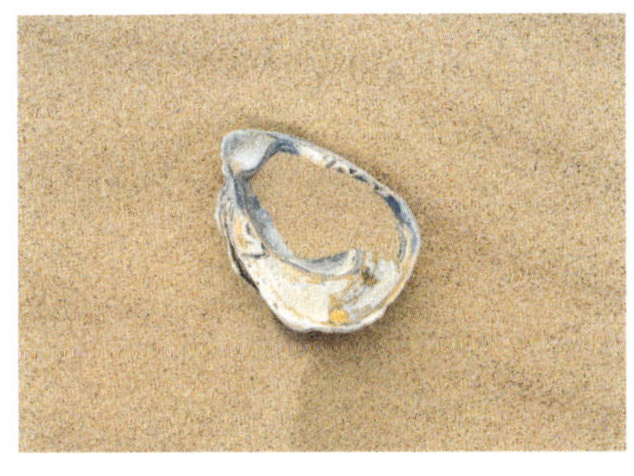

▲ *Geology and geography plays a big part in what features, plants, and animals can be found along a particular stretch of coastline.*

MACRO NOTES

A polarizing filter can be used to reduce reflections on non-metallic surfaces, including water. However, the effect only works when the surface is roughly 35° to the filter. A polarizing filter has no effect when you're face-on to the subject. Polarizing filters can also be used to deepen the blue of the sky at 90° to the position of the sun.

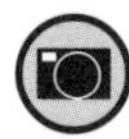

SPECIAL KIT

- Reversing ring

TIPS

- Lenses with a focal length between 28mm and 50mm work well coupled with a reversing ring.

- Use a step-up or step-down ring to fit lenses with different filter thread sizes to the reversing ring.

BACK TO FRONT

There are several ways to modify a non-macro lens so that it's able to shoot close-up images. Perhaps the most eccentric and counterintuitive is to reverse how it fits to the camera, so that the front element faces inward toward the sensor. This can be done very simply by holding the lens very carefully against the camera body. However, this is far from ideal and can make it awkward to hold the camera steady and fire the shutter button.

A better solution is to use a reversing ring, which is a metal lens mount that screws to the filter thread of the lens. You can then mount the lens back-to-front to the camera. When you buy a reversing ring, you therefore buy one that's designed for the lens mount of your camera and which has the correct filter thread for the lens you intend to reverse.

The main advantage to using reversing rings is that they're relatively inexpensive. The biggest disadvantage is that there are no electronic contacts between the lens and the camera. This means that selecting the required aperture can be a problem. Reversing rings are therefore better coupled with older, manual lenses that have an aperture ring. Your assignment is to try out a reversing ring to see how well it works with the lenses you own, then see what type of images can be shot and what level of magnification is possible.

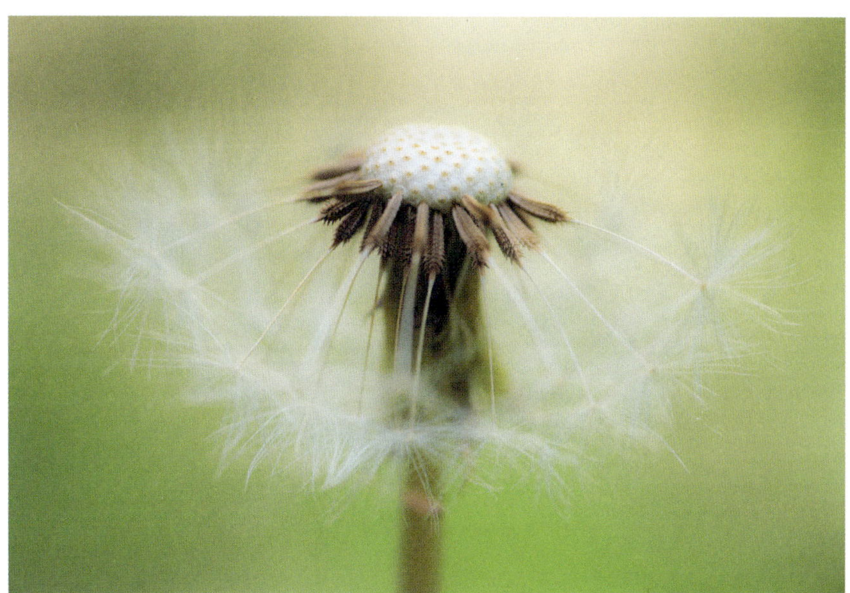

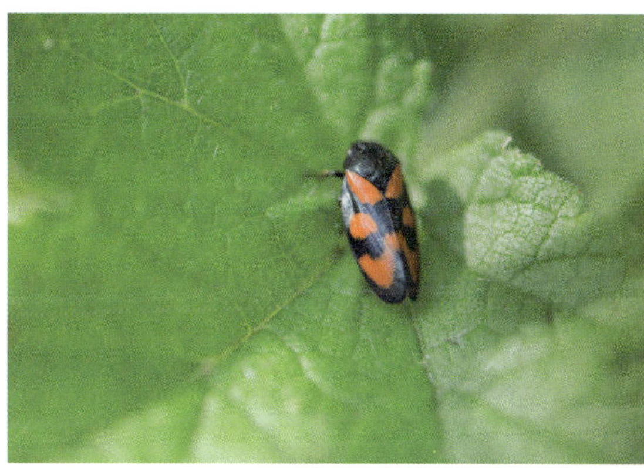

▲ *Modern lenses default to their widest aperture when not connected electronically to a camera. This will minimize depth of field, so focus precisely on the area you want to be sharpest.*

◄ *Live subjects such as insects will need to be very docile as a reversing ring will force you to get in close.*

MACRO NOTES

A true macro image is created when an image projected by a lens onto the sensor of a camera is life-sized or larger. This is often shown as a magnification figure such as 1x, for life-size, or 2x, which would be twice life-size. A lens with a magnification figure lower than 1, such as 0.5x or 0.25x, is therefore not a true macro lens. (The image projected by these two examples are half life-size and quarter life-size respectively.)

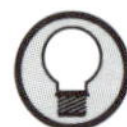 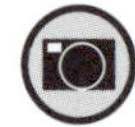

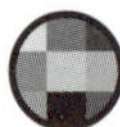 

TIPS

- Tracing or parchment paper, being translucent, can be used to soften a direct light source.

- Light from a flash can be softened either by a diffuser or by bouncing the light from a neutral surface—such as a ceiling—onto your subject.

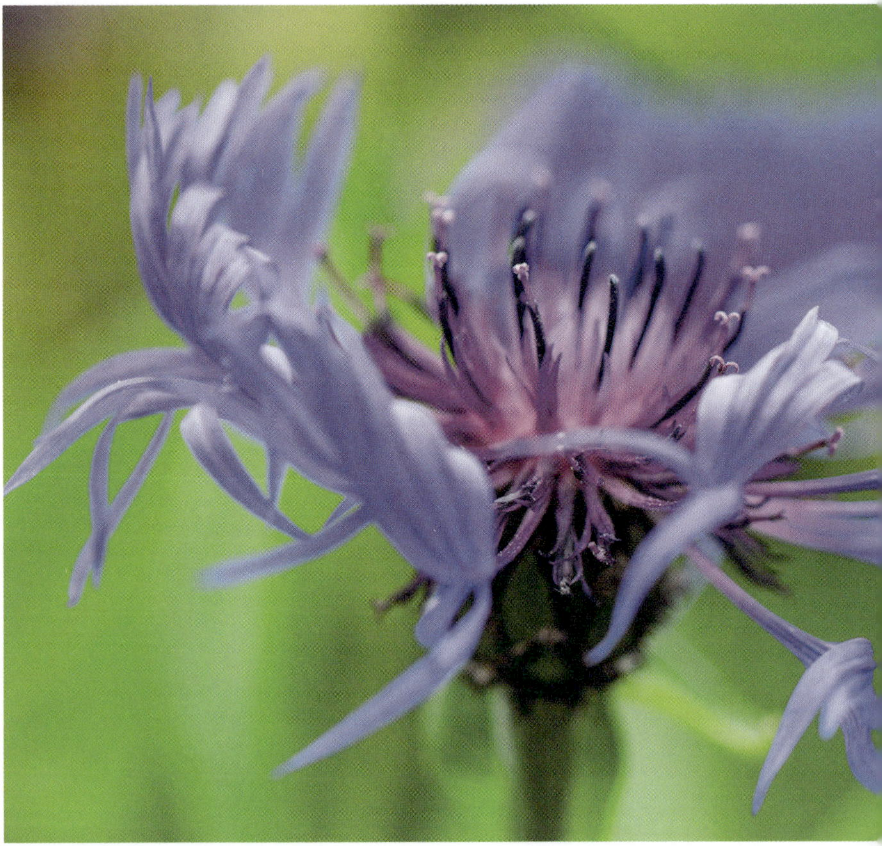

SOFTLY DOES IT

Light has many qualities such as color and intensity. Another quality is how soft a light source can be. (The opposite is a hard light source—see assignment 16.) Soft light is created when a light source is larger than the subject being illuminated. An overcast sky—when the sun is behind cloud—is a soft light source, for example.

Contrast in a scene lit by a soft light source is low. Shadows are bright and open, while the edges are diffuse. Highlights are also soft and often all but invisible, except on shiny or reflective objects. Not every subject suits soft lighting, however, but those that do include delicate natural subjects, such as flowers and insects.

For this assignment, shoot a variety of subjects in soft light, choosing those that you think would benefit from this type of lighting. Shoot the same subjects later in more direct lighting and compare the images to see if your initial judgment was correct.

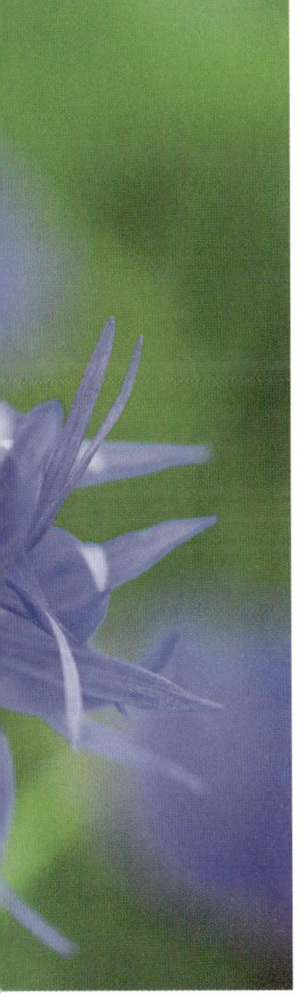

◄ *Soft light helps to reveal subtle color, which is often lost when a subject is lit directly.*

MACRO NOTES

Large reflectors can be used to shade a subject that would otherwise be lit by direct light. This will create a very soft, shadowless light, which is ideal for subjects like flowers. The shaded light will be biased more to blue, so the current White Balance preset may need to be altered, unless Auto WB is already selected.

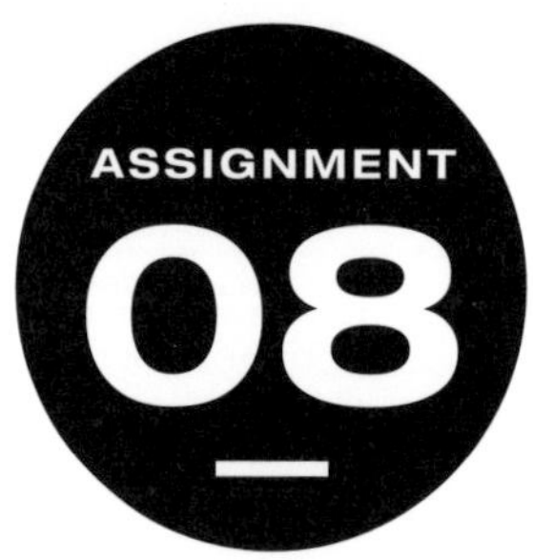

SPECIAL KIT

- Extension tubes

TIPS

- Extension tubes work with any lens, but for the best image quality, prime lenses are generally better than zooms.

- Extension tubes are small and light enough to leave in your camera bag permanently.

TAKING THE TUBE

Extension tubes are inexpensive accessories that fit between a camera and its lens. They alter the focus range of the lens, allowing it to focus closer than it was originally designed to do. However, there's no gain without a small amount of pain. In this case, the lens will no longer be able to focus on infinity. If you want to switch from shooting macro to shooting landscapes then you'll need to remove the extension tube first.

Extension tubes are essentially just hollow metal or plastic tubes with no optical elements of their own. The simplest versions lack electronic contacts, which means that neither autofocus or aperture control is available. Auto extension tubes have electronic contacts that allow the lens and camera to communicate, giving you more control. They are the best option, but are more expensive.

For this assignment, experiment with a set of extension tubes. Use them separately and in combination with a variety of lenses. Not all lenses work optimally with extension tubes. Knowing what limitations there are to a particular lens/extension tube combination will help you shoot more effectively in the future.

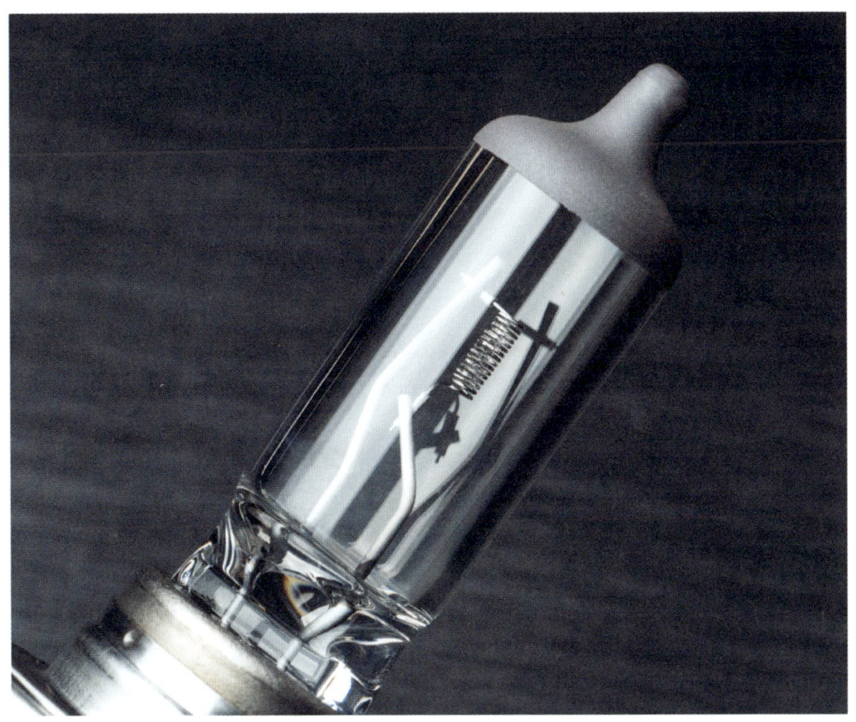

▲ *Extension tubes can be used with macro lenses but the gains in magnification will be relatively slight.*

ASSIGNMENT JOURNAL

MACRO NOTES

Extension tubes are usually sold as a set of three that can be used either in combination or separately. Generally, the shorter the focal length of a lens the less extension it will need to achieve 1x magnification. A telephoto lens will require so much extension to achieve 1x magnification that the technique is impractical, although the lens will still be able to focus more closely than without the use of extension tubes.

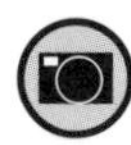
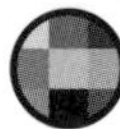

SPECIAL KIT

- Reflector or sheet of white paper or card
- Tripod

TIPS

- You can also use an open hand as a reflector if necessary.
- A black reflector subtracts light from shadows, reducing the light that falls on the subject.

▶ *A reflector was used here to prevent the shaded side of the subject from disappearing into the dark background.*

REFLECTED LIGHT

Controlling how light falls on a subject is an important element in the creation of a successful macro image. One piece of equipment that helps you do this is called a reflector. This is a sheet of material used to push light into the shadow areas of a scene and lower the contrast.

Most reflectors are made of a flexible and robust material and are available in a variety of sizes and finishes. White reflectors are the simplest type and don't add color to the reflected light. Silver reflectors are more efficient at reflecting light, although the result is a harder light that may be too intense for some subjects. Gold reflectors add warmth to the light being pushed into the shadows, which will be suitable for some subjects but is very much an aesthetic choice.

A sheet of white paper or card can also be used as a reflector and, for macro photography at least, is often a more convenient solution than a large photographic reflector. For this assignment select a subject in direct light. With your camera mounted on a tripod, shoot a sequence of images both with and without a reflector and compare the results.

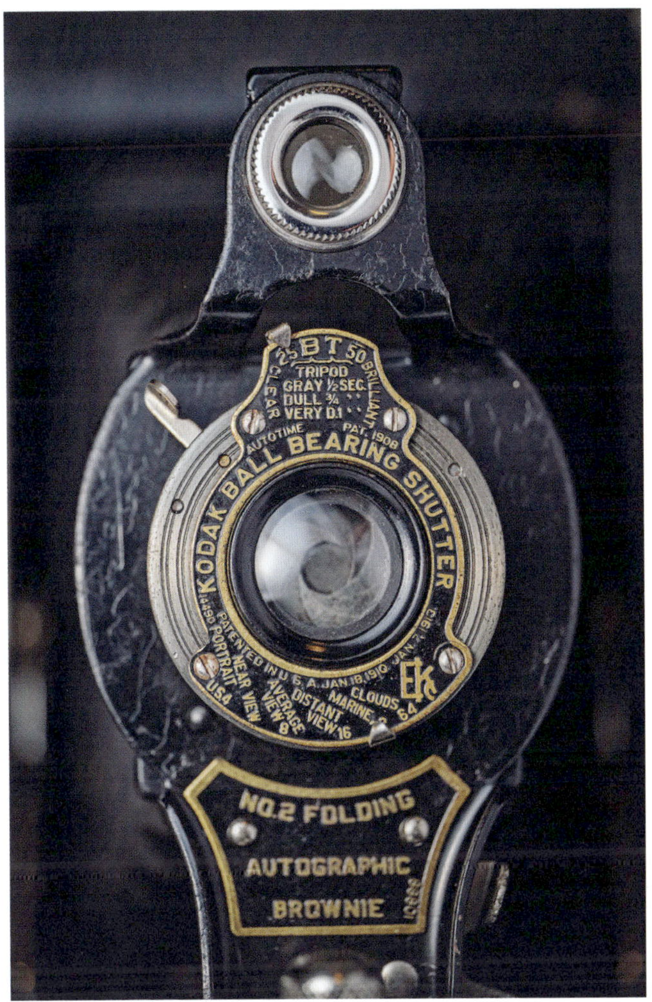

MACRO NOTES

A reflector is generally used when the subject is side-lit, with the reflector held out of shot on the shaded side. The effectiveness of the reflector is altered by changing its angle and distance relative to the subject. Reflectors can also be used to push light up from below. This is particularly useful when shooting subjects that shade light from above, such as fungi.

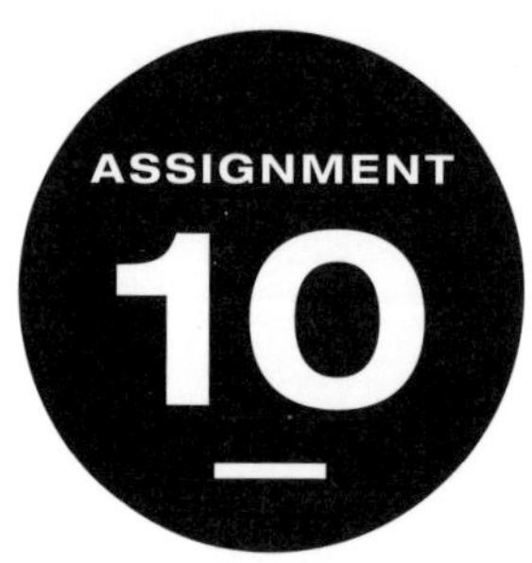

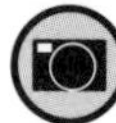
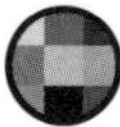

SPECIAL KIT

- Gardener's mat for kneeling on

TIPS

- Focus on the point of interest, such as the stamens or the edge of the petals.

- Keep the composition simple and backgrounds uncluttered.

- Gently move any distracting details out of the way, but don't remove or damage surrounding plants.

▶ *Shooting with a wide aperture has blurred the background, but required precise focusing on the flower.*

FLOWER POWER

Flowers are a popular subject for close-up and macro photography. There are so many different species of flowering plants that there are endless possibilities to create interesting and satisfying photos. Flowers are more easily found during the summer months, either growing wild or in cultivated gardens. There are fewer flowers to be found outside during the winter season, but houseplants or cut flowers are an acceptable alternative.

There are a number of challenges to shooting flowers, particularly outdoors. Smaller flowers are easily disturbed by even the slightest breeze. Using a windbreak is one solution, as is using a faster shutter speed to avoid blur. Flowers are often found close to the ground, so getting down low and shooting at their level will result in a more natural perspective. Flowers also benefit from being shot in soft light. Lightly overcast days work well as the light is softer but the intensity is still relatively high.

Your brief is to select a particular species of flower that is easily found locally. Shoot a variety of images and try to find different ways of composing as you do so. Vary the aperture and the depth-of-field to judge what effect this has on the results.

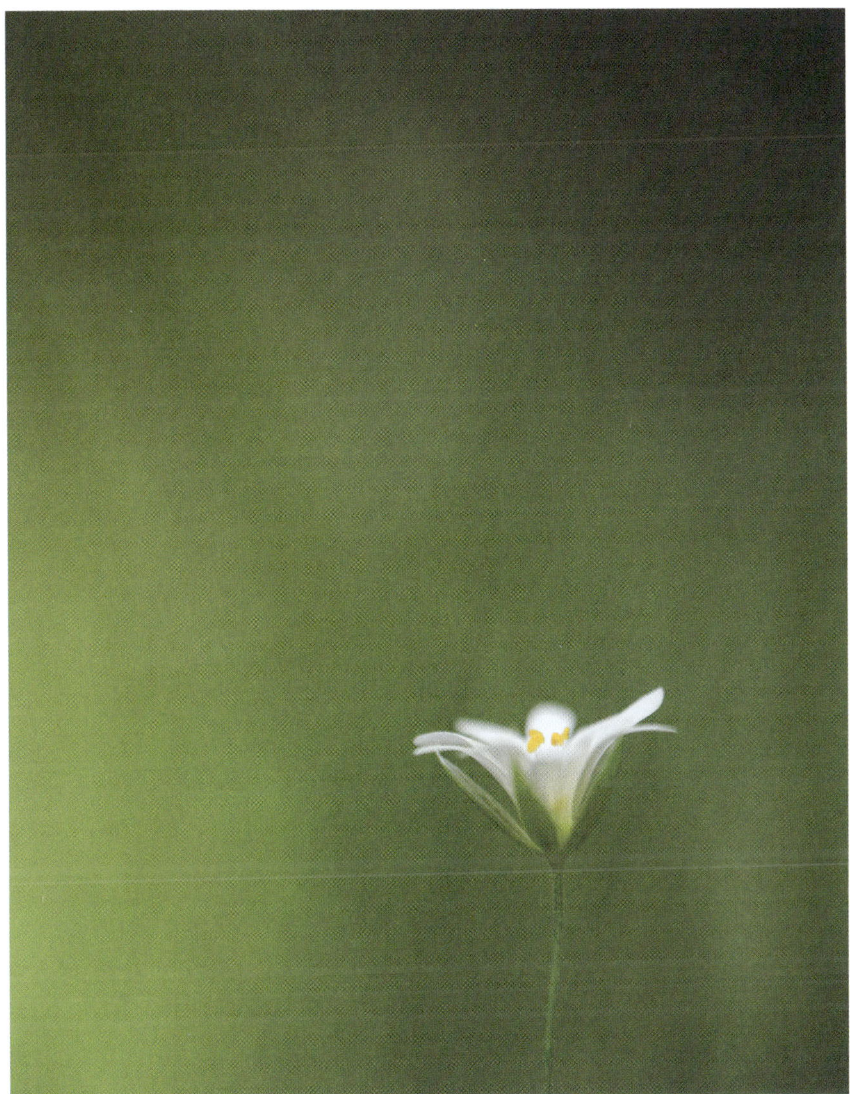

MACRO NOTES

Focus peaking is a focusing aid found on many DSLRs and mirrorless cameras. When selected, a colored outline is added to the sharpest areas of the LiveView image. The color of the outline can often be changed and selecting one that contrasts with the subject is recommended. Focus peaking is very useful when shooting macro, when manual focus is generally more useful than the camera's AF system.

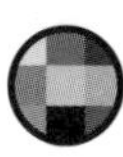

- Use the Manual exposure mode for full control over exposure.

- Shoot in LiveView and use the histogram to help assess the exposure. The histogram should be biased heavily to the left as your subject will be underexposed.

- Autofocus may struggle as the front of the subject will be extremely dark, so it's best to switch to manual focus.

SILHOUETTE

There are a number of ways to illuminate a scene. Arguably the most dramatic is backlighting. This is when the subject is placed directly between the camera and the light source. Backlighting is the ideal choice of lighting to create a silhouette, when the subject is grossly underexposed and no (or very few) details other than outline can be seen.

Ideally, the silhouetted subject should be readily identifiable from shape alone. Shooting from the same level as the subject will help to make it more recognizable. It should also stand alone within the scene for maximum impact. Anything that overlaps the subject will confuse its outline, making it harder to identify.

The simplest way to backlight a macro subject is to shoot against a bright sky, either outside or through a window. Other potential light sources include lightboxes, flashguns, or flashlights. For this assignment, set up a backlit scene. Experiment with exposure to see how this affects the results. Consider using postproduction to further increase contrast in your images.

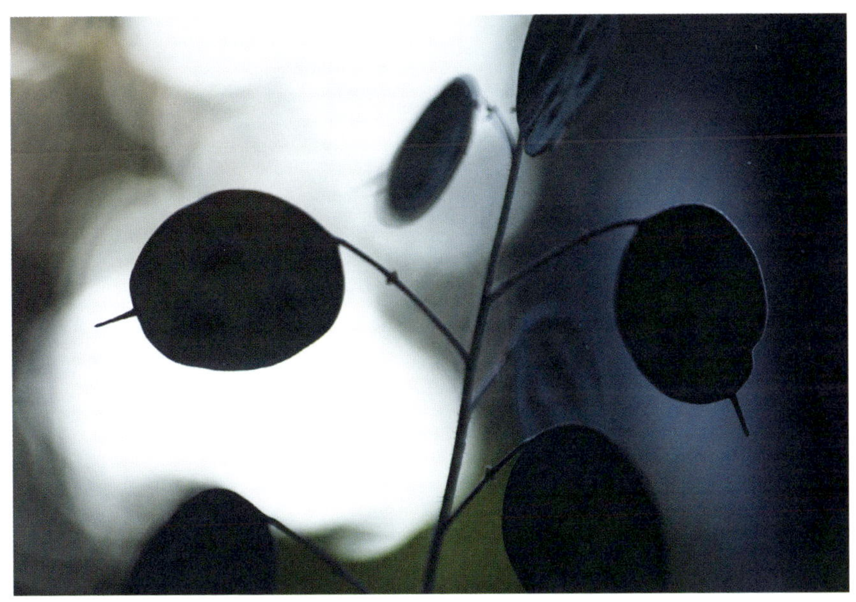

▲ *Use Highlight Alert to see when the highlights are burning out. Apply negative exposure compensation to darken the image.*

ASSIGNMENT JOURNAL

MACRO NOTES

A white light source will create very stark, graphic images, similar to the original paper cut-out portraits created by Étienne de Silhouette (after whom the technique is named). Using a colored light source will create more visual interest and can be used to add atmosphere to an image. Red, for instance, could be used to evoke a sunset or fire. Blue could be used to suggest night or cold. The key is to match the color to the subject so that there's a sensible connection.

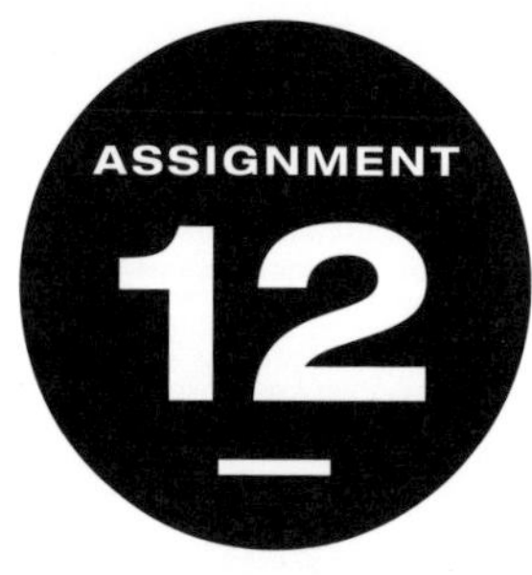

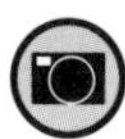

TIPS

- Muted colors are more minimal than bright primary colors.

- High- or low-key lighting can be used to create minimalistic images (see assignments 27 and 35).

SINGLED OUT

Your brief here is to create a set of images that are minimalist, but still visually interesting. A cluttered image with no obvious focal point or subject is hard to read and visually confusing. Keeping composition simple but meaningful will result in a much stronger image. Less is usually very definitely more.

A simple composition typically has only one focal point or subject. The visual interest in the composition is therefore often dependent on where the subject is placed in the image space (unless the subject fills the image space completely). There's no hard and fast rule on how to do this, although intuition is often a good guide—if it feels right then it probably is.

Simple images may still have other elements in the image but these should be there only to support the subject and not overwhelm it. Using a limited depth-of-field (often unavoidable in macro photography anyway) can help to throw potentially distracting elements out of focus and make them less obvious. Carefully consider the types of subjects you shoot. These will need to hold a viewer's attention and so requires some visual appeal, whether that's because they're quirky, colorful, unusual, or visually arresting.

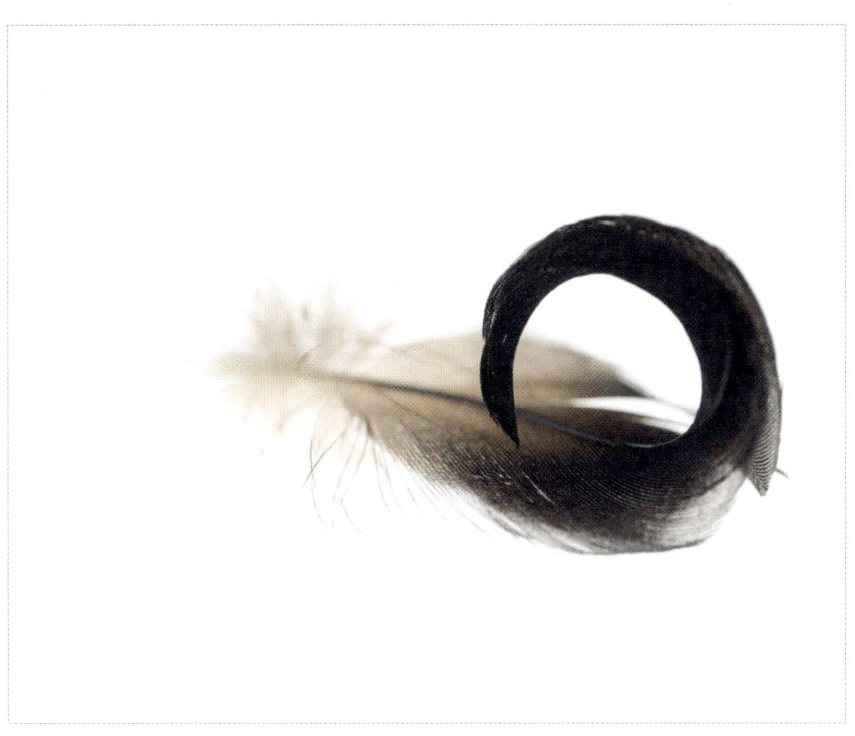

MACRO NOTES

Visual weight describes how "heavy"—or eye-catching—something is in an image.
A person's face is visually heavy, for example. Colors have different weights too.
Warm colors, such as reds and oranges, are heavy and leap out more than cooler colors,
such as blue and green. Words, letters, and numbers are visually heavy and potentially
distracting if not the main focal point. Thinking about visual weight is a good way to decide
whether something should stay in an image or whether it's better excluded.

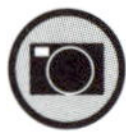

TIPS

- Add color to shiny metallic objects by holding pages from magazines over them.

- Shoot from an angle you'd not normally view the subject from.

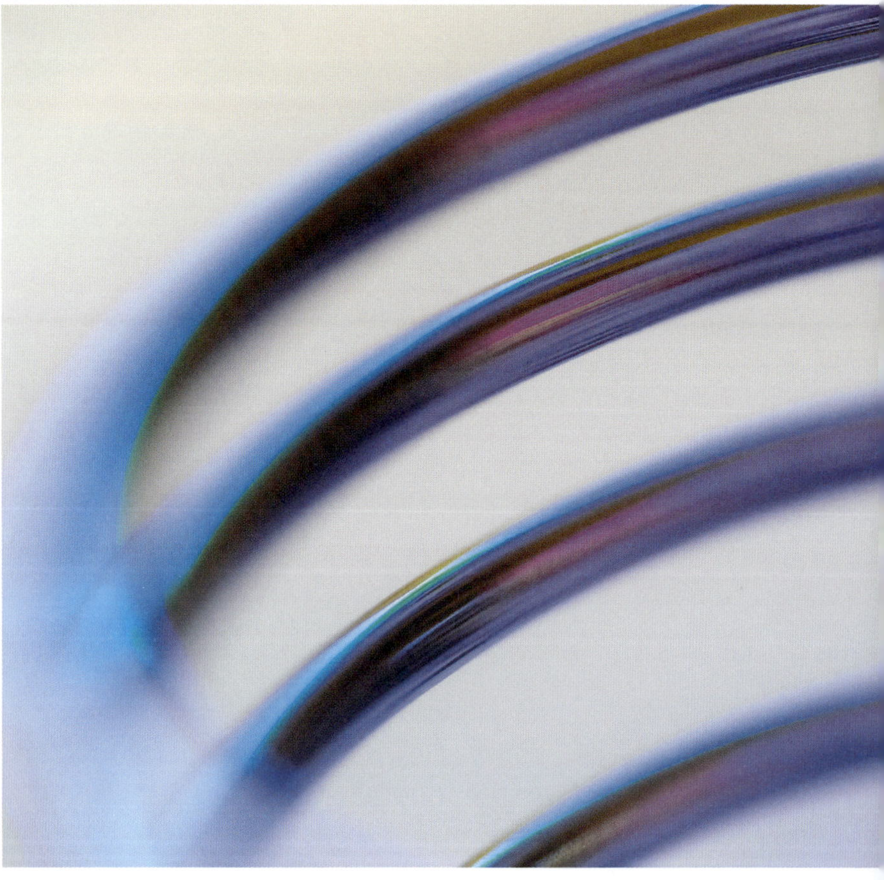

ABSTRACTS

An abstract photo is one that relies entirely on shape, color, or texture for its effect. The subject of the photo—even though it's an object you may see every day—is often not readily identifiable (at least not immediately). Macro photography is ideally suited to the creation of abstract imagery. Getting in close is a very effective and simple way of make a visually intriguing image of something that's otherwise very ordinary.

For this assignment, collect together a small selection of household objects and shoot them in an abstract way. Look for repetitive patterns, shapes, lines, and colors that will help make the images visually satisfying. Think about how you light your objects too. Lighting, through the creation of shadows and highlights, can be used to increase the sense of abstraction by hiding identifiable details or revealing otherwise invisible texture. The result should be a set of compelling and artistically pleasing images.

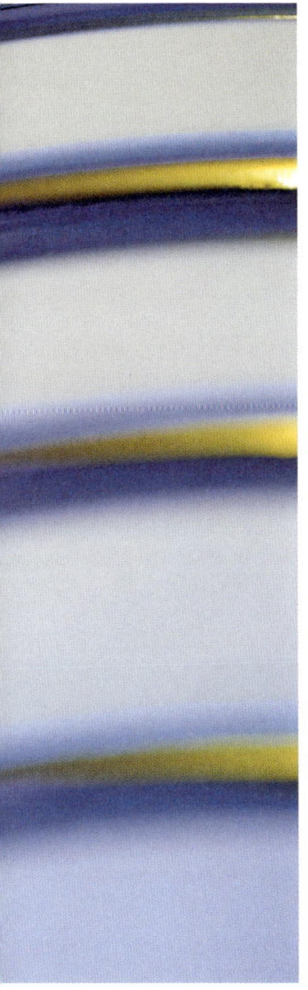

◄ *Using a wide aperture to restrict depth-of-field further abstracted this image of a metal egg cup.*

MACRO NOTES

Macro photography tends to reveal blemishes that aren't visible to the naked eye. Dust in particular is often annoyingly visible in macro shots. Blemishes can be removed in postproduction but that will take far longer than a quick clean of your subject prior to shooting. Use a lint-free cloth to clean substantial objects or a small paintbrush or blower brush on more delicate items.

 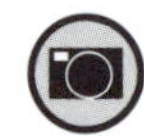

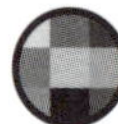 

SPECIAL KIT

- Polarizer

- Sheet of polarizing film

- A thin clear plastic object

- Tablet or phone

- Tripod

- Lightbox

TIPS

- Use plastic objects that are free of scratches and dust, or remove blemishes in postproduction.

- Set your camera's Picture Style to Vivid to create images with highly saturated colors.

- Consider how you place your subjects within the image space and compose so that there is nothing distracting in the shot.

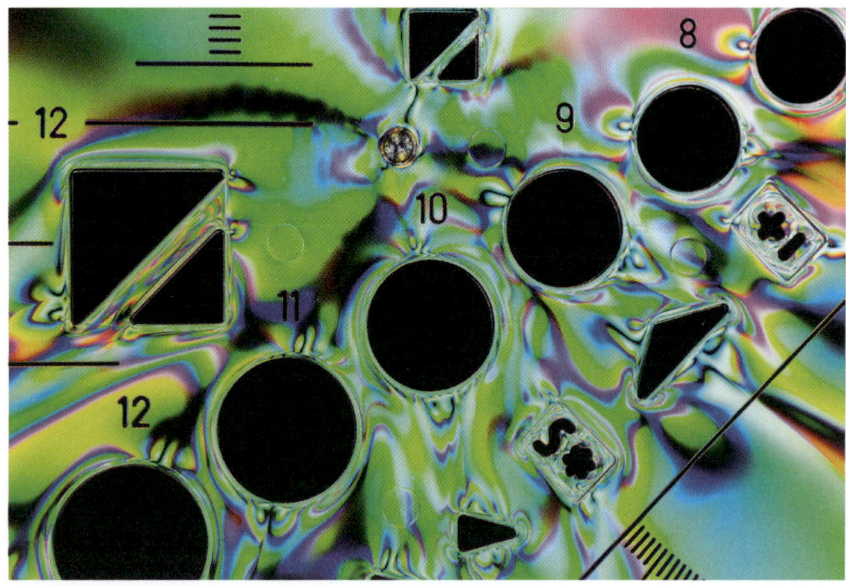

RAINBOW COLORS

Cross-polarization reveals the points of stress in backlit clear plastic objects, creating a full spectrum of colors where none were previously visible. The technique is a great way to create very striking abstract imagery from otherwise mundane household objects.

The cross-polarization effect is variable, and the results largely depend on the subject and the amount of cross-polarization applied. The fun is in the experimentation, as the results are hard to predict beforehand. Use your judgment to shoot when the colors and patterns are most pleasing.

For this assignment, find three or more clear plastic objects from around your home. Ideally use objects that are thin, completely transparent, and that can be laid flat, such as a plastic ruler or cutlery. Shoot a range of images, varying the amount of cross-polarization and adjusting the placement of the subject in the shots. Try combining two or more objects in the same image, arranging them in interesting ways within the image space. Use postproduction to enhance color and contrast.

◀ *At a certain point in the rotation of the polarizer the backlit light source will appear to turn black.*

THE PROCESS

1   Fit the polarizer to the lens on your camera.

2   Switch on the lightbox and place the polarizing film (or a second polarizer) on the lightbox. Alternatively, use a tablet or phone displaying a white screen instead of the lightbox and film.

3   Place the plastic object on the film (or tablet screen).

4   Position your camera directly above the object and slowly rotate the polarizer fitted to the lens.

5   Adjust exposure if necessary and then shoot.

▶ Using Auto WB will help to keep colors accurate when shooting under the mixed lighting setups used in museums.

MACRO IN MUSEUMS

Museums are great places for close-up and macro photography (when photography is allowed). The sheer range of exhibits on display will usually be enough to satisfy any photographer. However, this doesn't mean that shooting images in museums is easy.

Most exhibits in museums are behind protective glass. Any reflections in the glass will be recorded by the camera, creating visual distractions. The simplest way to overcome the problem is to press the lens gently against the glass. A second problem is minimum focusing distance: the lens may not be able to focus on exhibits close to the front of a display, particularly if you're holding the lens against the glass. The lighting conditions may also be less than ideal and using your own lighting in the form of flash will probably be frowned upon. With imagination these challenges can be overcome, opening up a whole new range of subjects for your macro photography.

Your assignment is to shoot a themed set of photos at your local museum (check with the museum if this is permissible first). Work through any problems you may have, thinking up creative solutions, if necessary, particularly if a straight shot of a potential subject is impossible.

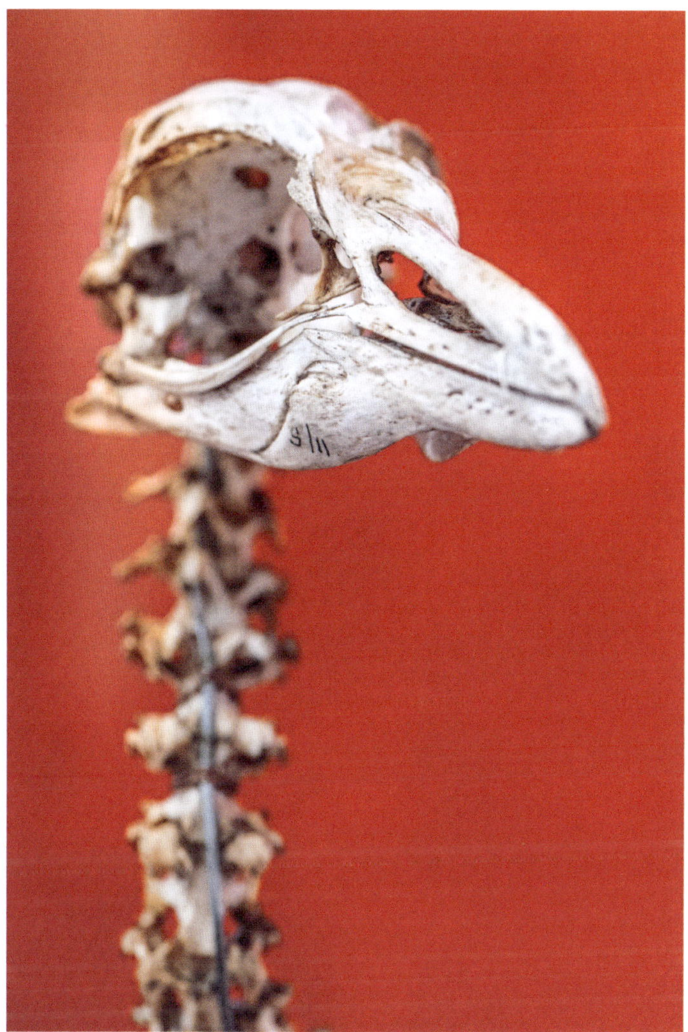

MACRO NOTES

The minimum focusing distance of a lens (including macro lenses) is measured from the focal plane inside the camera, which lines up with where the sensor is mounted. It is marked on the camera body by the ⦵. Generally, a short focal length macro lens will have a smaller focusing distance than a macro lens with a longer focal length. This makes short focal length macro lenses easier to use when shooting in places like museums.

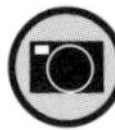

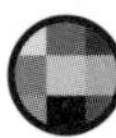

TIPS

- Black and white images work well shot with hard light (see assignment 45).

- Areas of deep shadow can cause a camera to overexpose. Use negative exposure compensation to avoid this if necessary.

MACRO NOTES

Point light sources can cause flare, usually seen as blobs of color across the image space or a reduction in contrast. Lens hoods help reduce the risk of flare from point light sources outside the image space, but aren't so effective when a point light source shines directly at the lens.

HARD LIGHT

A light is hard when the light source is smaller relative to the subject being illuminated. Although the sun is far bigger that the earth, the apparent size of the sun in the sky is small. On a cloudless day the light from the sun is therefore hard. Point light sources, such as unshaded household bulbs, also create a hard lighting effect.

The visual characteristics of hard light are intensely bright highlights and deep shadows with sharply-defined edges. Hard light is ideal illumination for objects with a well-defined geometric shape. It is less well suited to softer, natural shapes with less well-defined edges or forms.

To complete this assignment, shoot a number of subjects in hard light, carefully selecting those that you think would work well under this kind of illumination. To create hard lighting use a desk lamp, flashlight, or direct flash. If contrast is too high, add light into the shadows with a reflector.

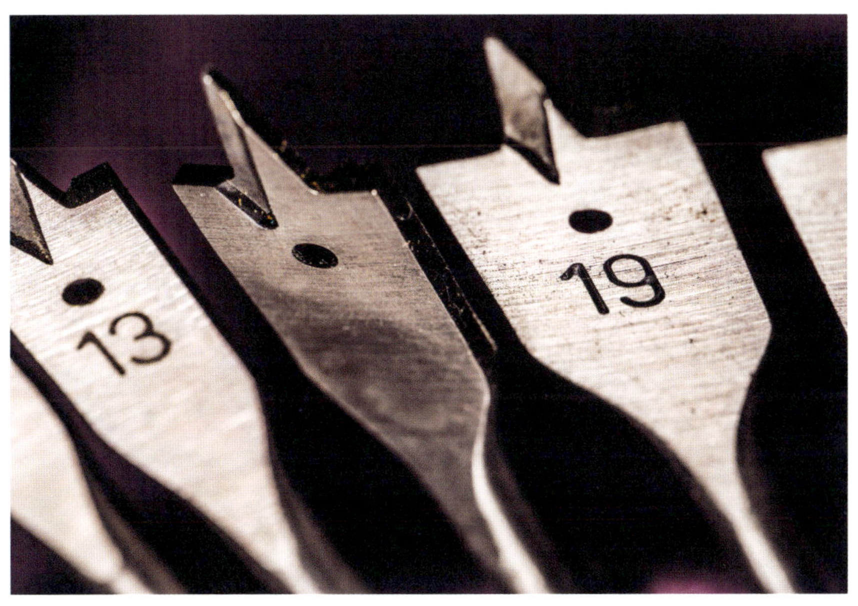

▲ *A direct, hard light helps to emphasize the sharp-edged nature of subjects like tools.*

ASSIGNMENT JOURNAL

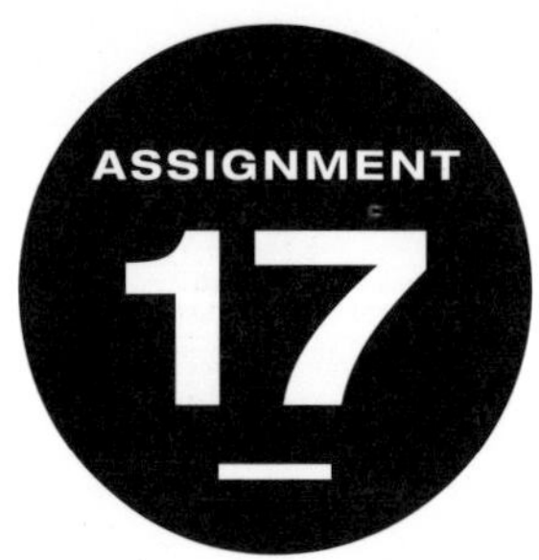

ASSIGNMENT
17

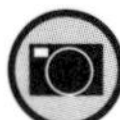

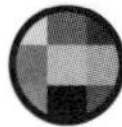

TIPS

- Increase the distance between the subject and the background to make the background as blurred as possible.

- Stopping the lens down by one or two stops will make the background less blurred, but can help improve the quality of out-of-focus highlights.

ASSIGNMENT JOURNAL

MACRO NOTES

Another way to affect the quality of bokeh is to cut a small shape out of a piece of thick card and hold the card against the front element of the lens. Any out-of-focus highlights will then take on the shape you made. Star and crescent moon shapes work well as they are instantly recognizable.

▶ *Light dappled through foliage is effectively multiple point light sources.*

BOKEHLICIOUS

Bokeh is a Japanese word used to describe the aesthetic quality of any out-of-focus areas in an image. The quality of bokeh is important when shooting with a lens set to its maximum aperture, particularly with a telephoto or macro lens. This is when depth-of-field will be minimized and typically only the subject is sharp.

"Good" bokeh results in near-circular out-of-focus highlights without hard edges, and smooth transitions between one region of an image and another. ("Bad" bokeh is harsh, and out-of-focus highlights are distorted or textured with an "onion ring" effect.) The quality of bokeh is determined by the design of the lens in use. The most important factor is the shape the aperture makes; a more rounded aperture typically produces more pleasing bokeh than an aperture that is polygonal in shape.

Macro photography is an ideal way to experiment with bokeh as depth-of-field is usually very limited. For this assignment shoot a short series of images using the maximum aperture of your macro lens. Choose your background carefully. Experiment with small point light sources such as Christmas tree lights to create your out-of-focus highlights, for example.

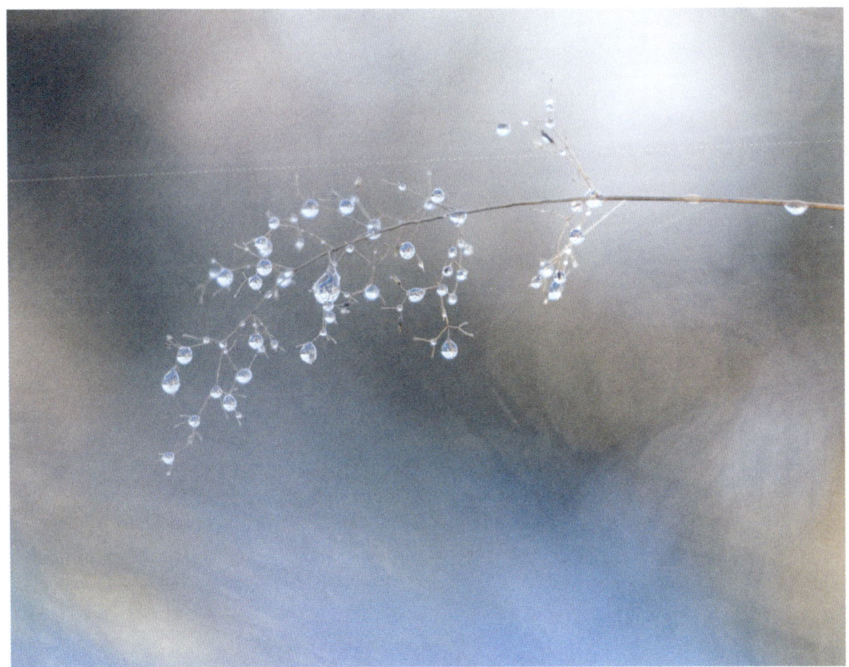

- Use a small aperture to ensure that all the important elements of the story are in focus.

- Use lighting to convey mood: a humorous story will benefit from being brightly lit, whereas somber lighting would suit a more serious approach.

MAKING A SCENE

People respond to stories, whether that's in the form of words or a single picture. Although macro photography isn't the obvious medium for creating a story, it can be done with careful thought and a few pertinent props. A picture that tells a story is one that can be understood quickly and clearly, such as a cartoon.

People are usually the subjects of stories, which is an impossibility when shooting macro images. Or is it? Toy figures make a good stand-in for real people when creating a story in picture form. Figures used to decorate model train dioramas are realistic and readily available, and can be bought in a variety of poses. One possibility is combining toy figures with common household objects that have a visual or conceptual link.

For this assignment, create a short series of visual stories. These could be humorous, serious, or just plain surreal. Have fun creating these stories. Share them with others to see how they respond. The only limit is your imagination.

MACRO NOTES

Light tents (also known as studio boxes) are generally used for product photography. A light tent is a wireframe cube covered on four sides by thin white fabric. Light that passes through the fabric is diffused so that anything placed within the tent is softly lit. (The front side is open so that you can point your camera into the interior space.) Light tents are ideal for projects that require consistent lighting for a sequence of photos.

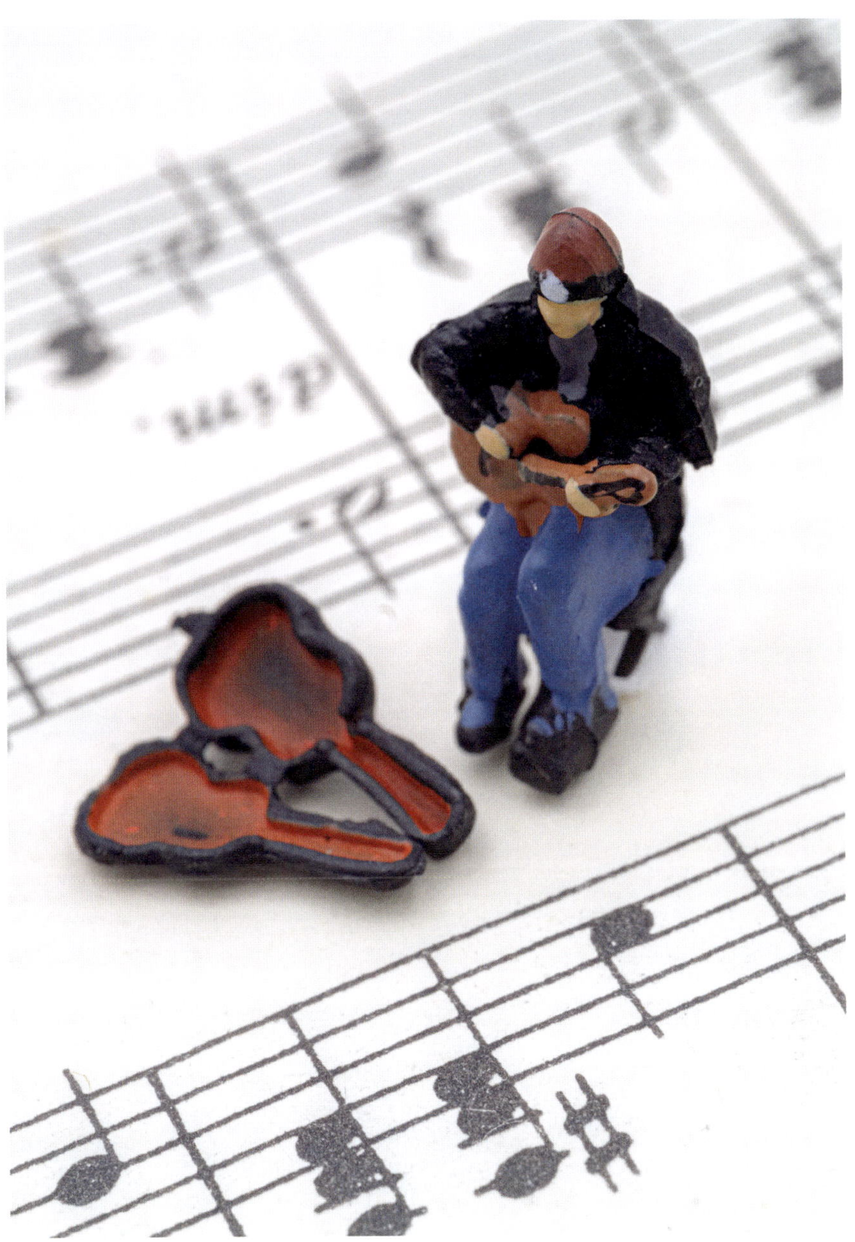

▲ The background you choose is as
important as the subject in setting the
scene for your story.

TIPS

- Direct light—whether the sun or from a flash—will add sparkle to the ice crystals.

- When shooting in shade use the Daylight White Balance preset to retain a cool blue look.

- Reflective white frost can cause underexposure. Add one to two stops of positive exposure compensation if this happens.

▶ *The earthy tones of leaf litter create an interesting visual contrast to bone-white ice crystals.*

FROSTY CLOSE-UPS

Natural macro subjects can be found during every season. Winter brings the chance of frost, which adds a photogenic sheen of ice crystals to outdoor objects and creates interesting fern-like patterns on glass. Frost typically forms during the night when there is little or no cloud in the sky and when the temperature drops and stays below 32°F/0°C. A local weather forecast is the best way to find out whether this is likely to happen.

Hoar frost is a particularly beautiful form of frost, caused when airborne water vapor comes into contact with an already frozen object. Grass and trees covered in hoar frost look as though they've been dipped in sugar. The effect doesn't last long and even feeble winter sunshine will soon cause the frost to melt.

Your brief is to shoot a series of macro shots of frost-covered objects. These can be either artificial or natural, but should work as a coherent collection of images.

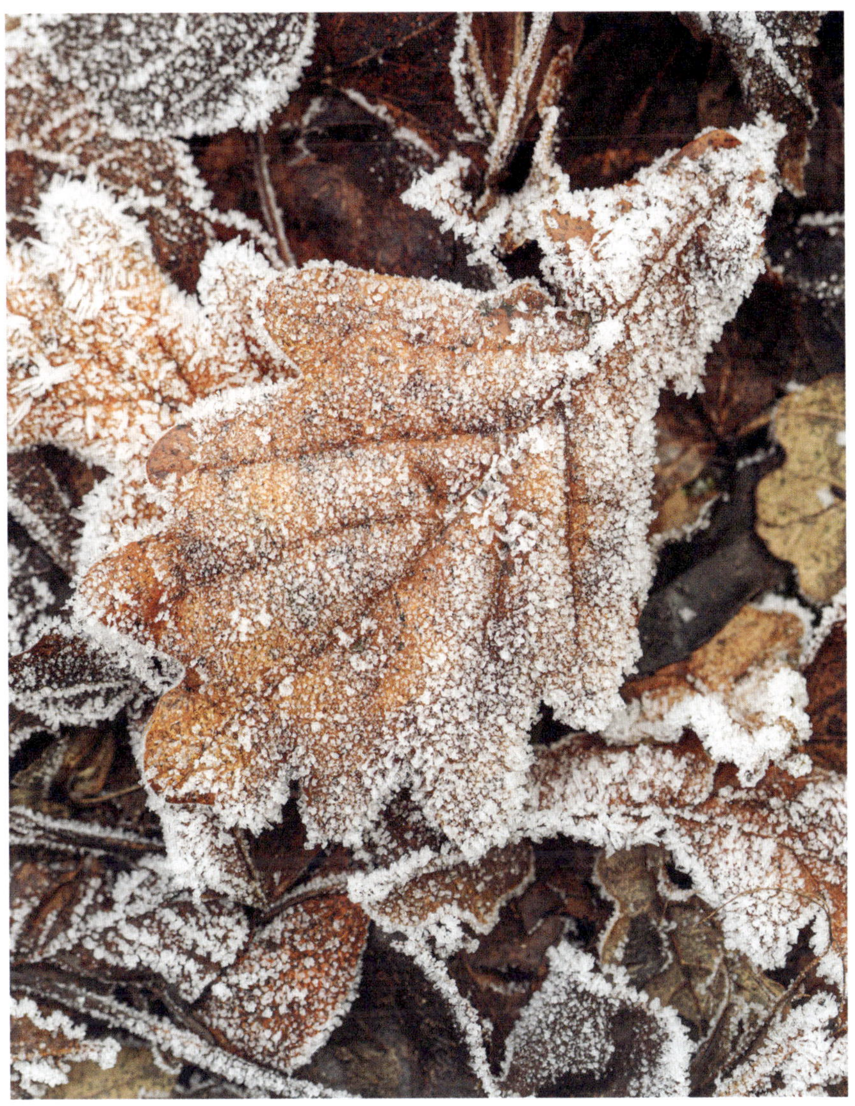

MACRO NOTES

Cold has a detrimental effect on battery life, causing them to deplete more rapidly than normal. Make sure that your camera batteries are all fully charged before venturing outdoors. Keep spare batteries in an inside pocket of your jacket where they can stay warm until needed.

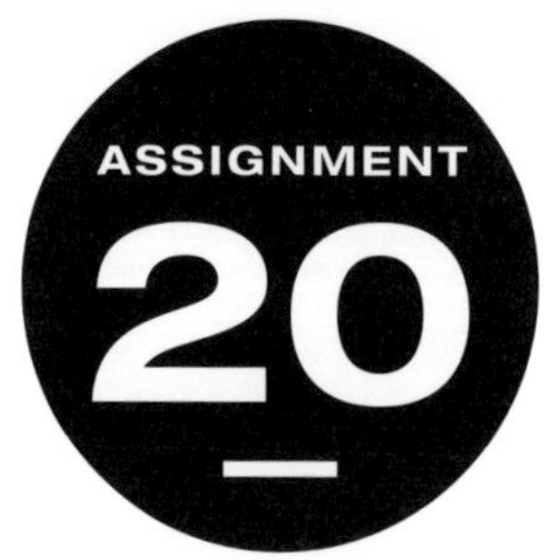

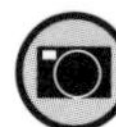

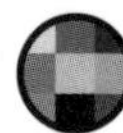

SPECIAL KIT

- Tripod

- Clamp or clothes peg

- Black background

TIPS

- Use a clamp to hold the match in position.

- Use a longer length macro lens to distance the camera from the heat. Or shoot farther back and crop in later.

- Work in a well-ventilated room and keep a damp cloth handy to smother any sparks.

FLAME ON

Flame is a fascinating and vibrantly colorful photographic subject. Matches can be used to generate a small and controllable flame suitable for macro photography. What's so wonderful about using matches is that they go through several different—if brief—stages as they light. There's an initial flare as the chemicals ignite followed by a steady flame that gradually diminishes as they burn down. Each stage is visually different, which can be used to create an interesting sequence of shots.

Shooting a match's flame doesn't have to be done in complete darkness, although a nonreflective dark or black background will help the flame stand out more. A sheet of black velvet placed roughly a meter behind the match is ideal. Some light on the match will help to define its shape. Off-camera flash set to low power and placed to the side of the match works well to illuminate the wooden shaft.

For this assignment, create a short series of match flame photos (explained overleaf). Vary the composition and exposure between shots until you have an interesting sequence. Have fun with the assignment, making sure you stay safe as you do so.

▶ *This was my favorite from a sequence of thirty shots, as it had the most pleasing flame shape.*

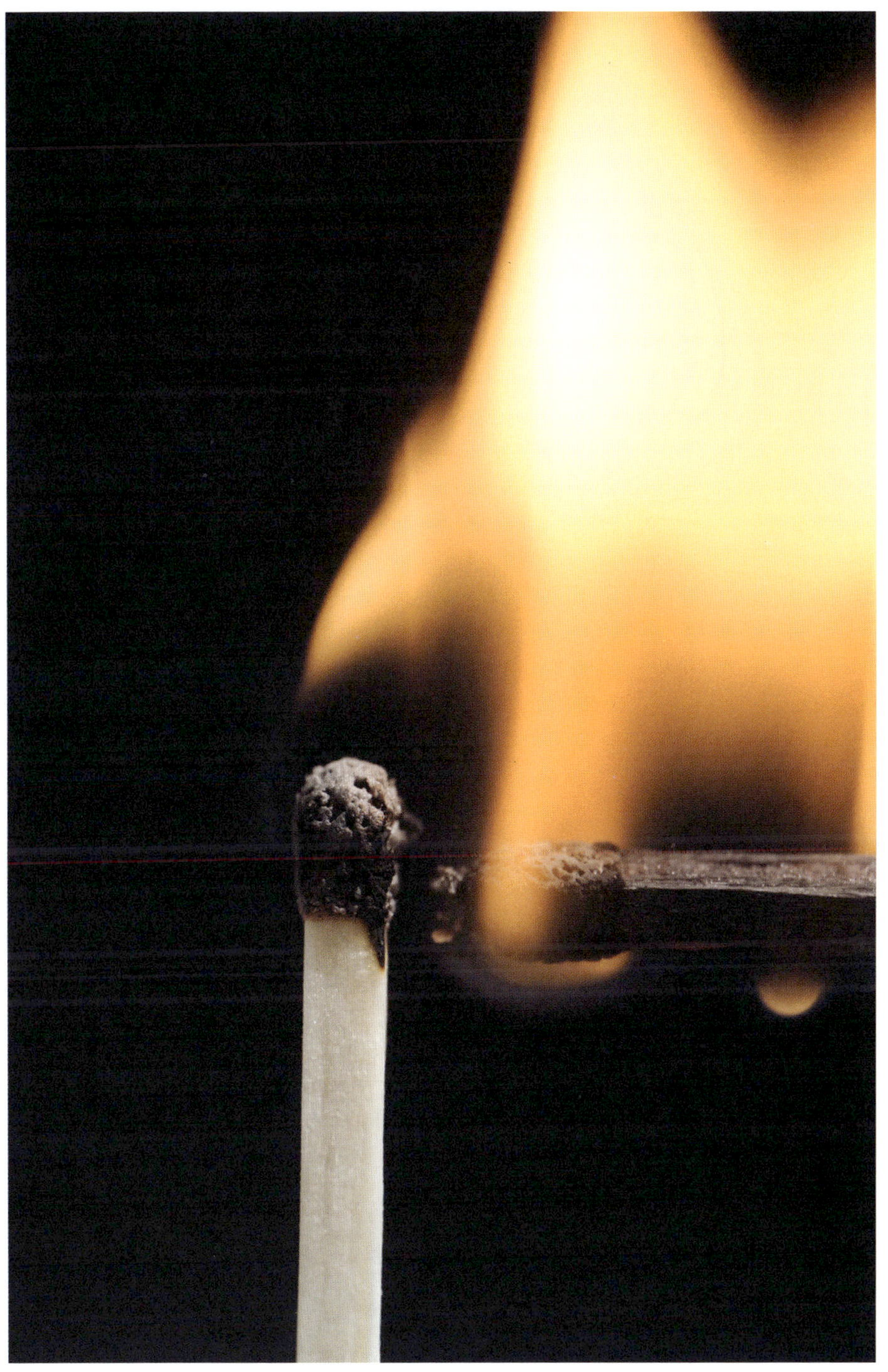

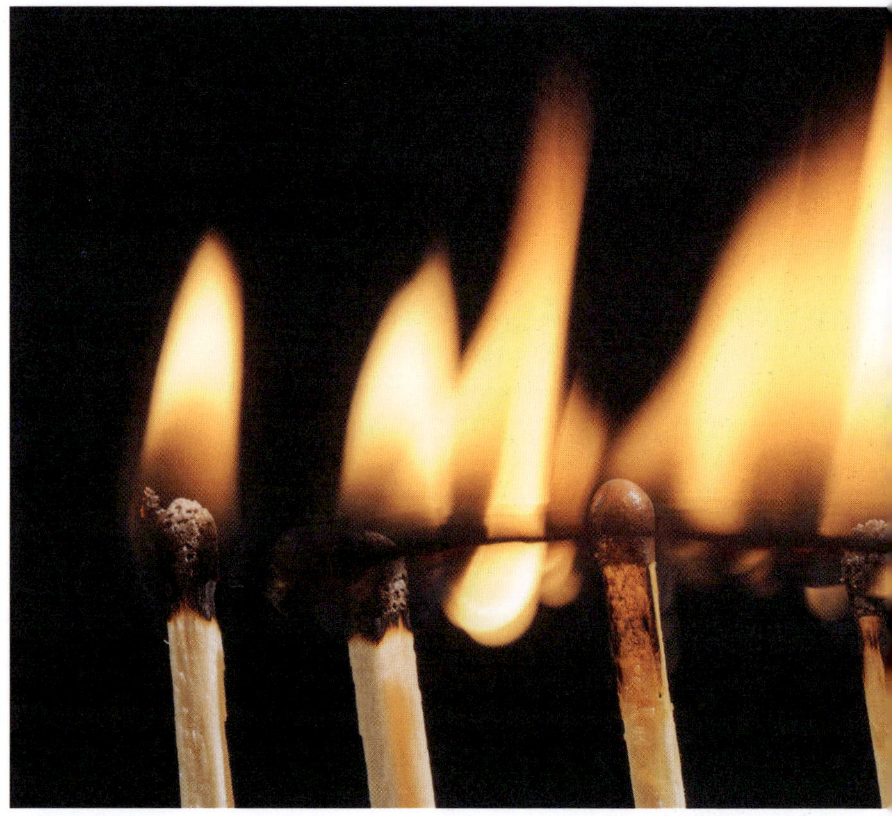

THE PROCESS

1 Clamp your match into position on a flat stable surface.

2 Position your camera on a tripod, level with the match. Have a box of matches close by.

3 Manually focus on the tip of the match.

4 With the camera in Manual exposure mode, set the aperture to f/8 to f/11, the ISO to 100 to 200, and the shutter speed to 1/400 sec.

5 Select the Continuous shooting drive mode.

6 Use a second match to light your subject match and start shooting just before you do so to capture the initial flaring. This is easier if someone is able to help or by using a remote release.

7 Stop shooting once the flame is steady and the match begins to burn down.

8 Review the images and reshoot, altering the exposure if necessary.

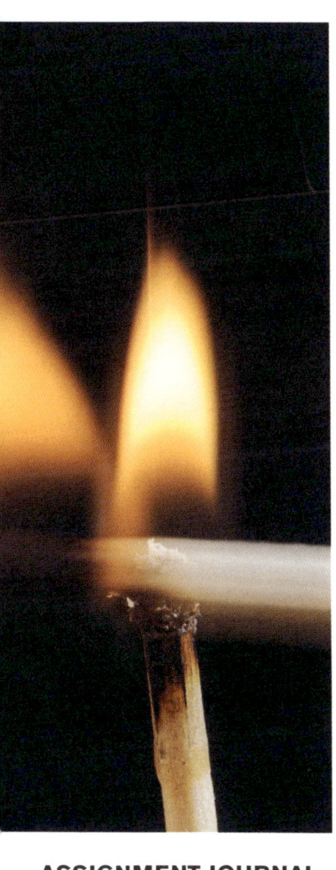

◀ *To fill a horizontal frame use multiple matches, keeping the line of matches parallel to the camera.*

ASSIGNMENT JOURNAL

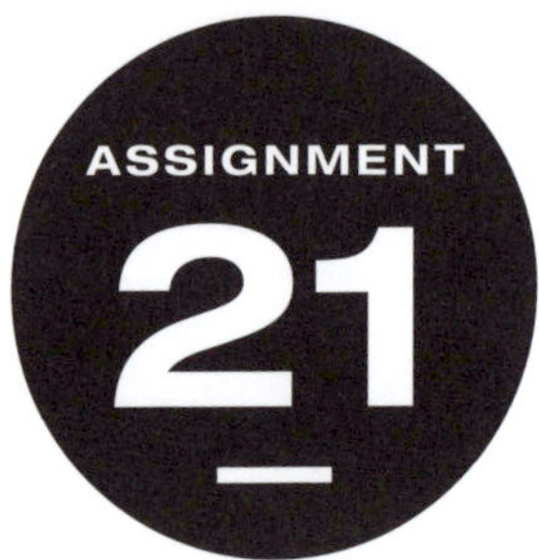

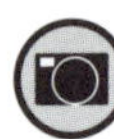

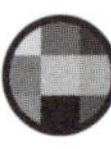

SPECIAL KIT

- Tripod

- Lamp or off-camera flash

- Black background

TIPS

- Use a geological guide for your local area to search for fossils.

- Use a blower to blow dust and dirt from the fossil before you shoot.

▼ *Focus on the most important part of the fossil, such as the eyes of this trilobite.*

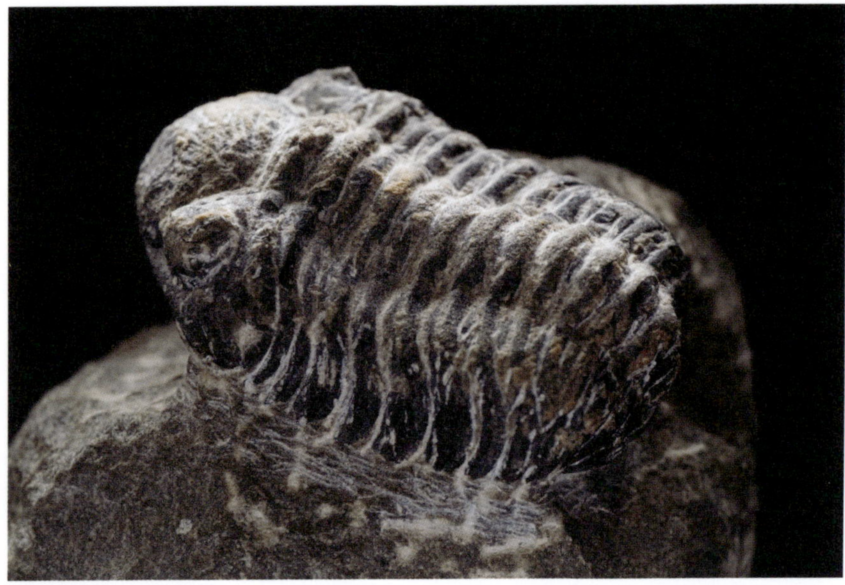

FOSSILS

Fossils are the physical evidence of organisms that were alive thousands, millions, even billions of years ago. Use the word fossil and most people think of the mineralized remains of plants or animals encased in rock. However, fossils can also be the traces left behind by an organism, such as footprints or their droppings, known as coprolites. Fossils are interesting macro subjects and are readily found in sedimentary rock layers.

Out of context, the scale of a fossil can be hard to judge from a photo. Adding a familiar object to the shot—such as a coin—is a simple way to reveal the size of the fossil. An alternative is to hold the fossil, though this does require a very steady hand unless the shutter speed is sufficiently fast.

How you light the fossil is important. Perfectly flat fossils can be shot in soft lighting. Three-dimensional fossils will require more direct lighting to create a sense of depth. Side lighting will create shadows and highlights and reveal the details of the fossil.

Your brief for this assignment is to shoot a fossil in a number of different ways. If you don't own any fossils and don't know where to find any, then your local museum may be an option. Think about composition and lighting as you shoot. A straight record shot will be useful as a reference, but also try more artistic approaches too.

MACRO NOTES

Matching the White Balance to the light source ensures that the color of the fossil will be rendered accurately. Presets such as Flash are a good starting point, but a custom White Balance will be more accurate still. The technique varies between camera brands but typically involves shooting a test shot of a neutrally-colored surface, placed in the same light as the subject. This shot is then used to create the custom White Balance.

ASSIGNMENT JOURNAL

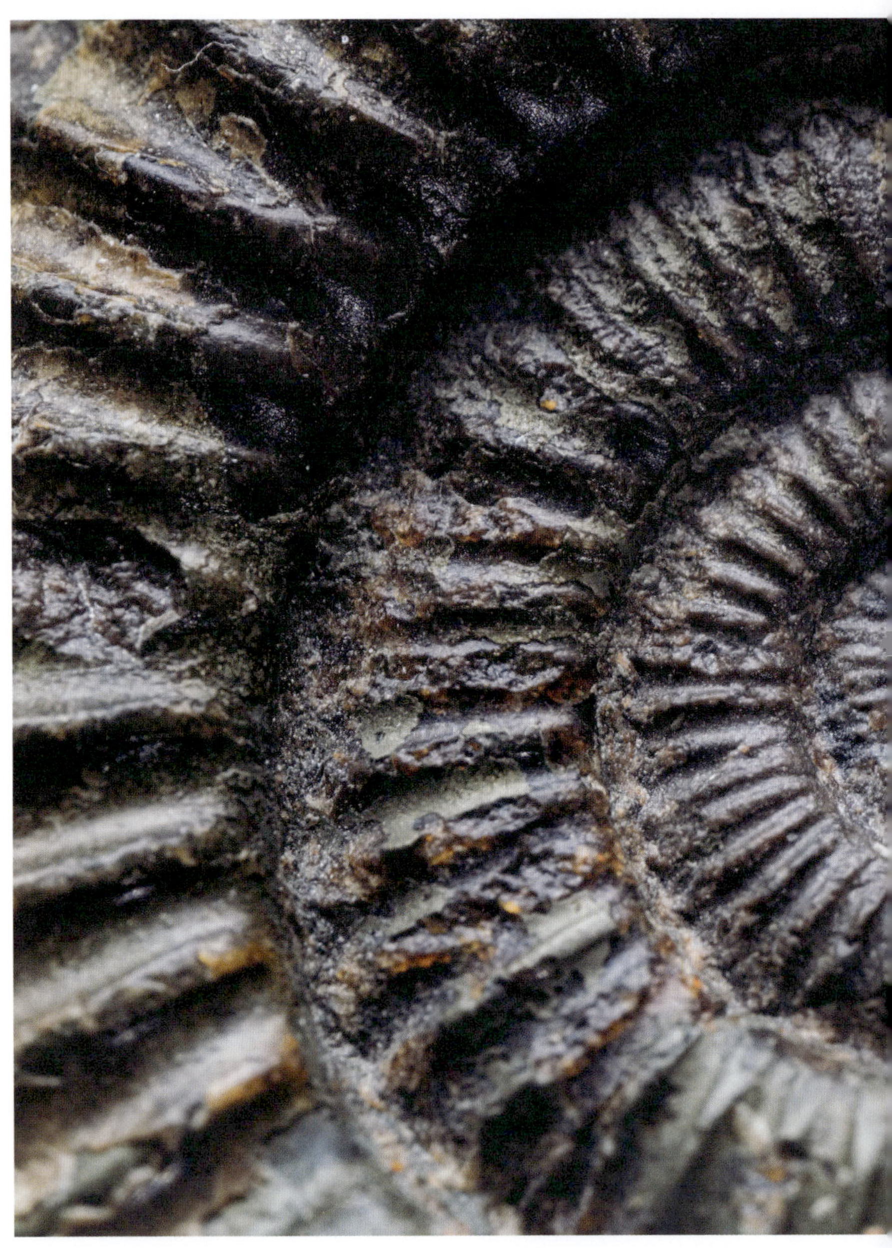

▲ *Use the fossil's natural shapes and lines to guide your composition.*

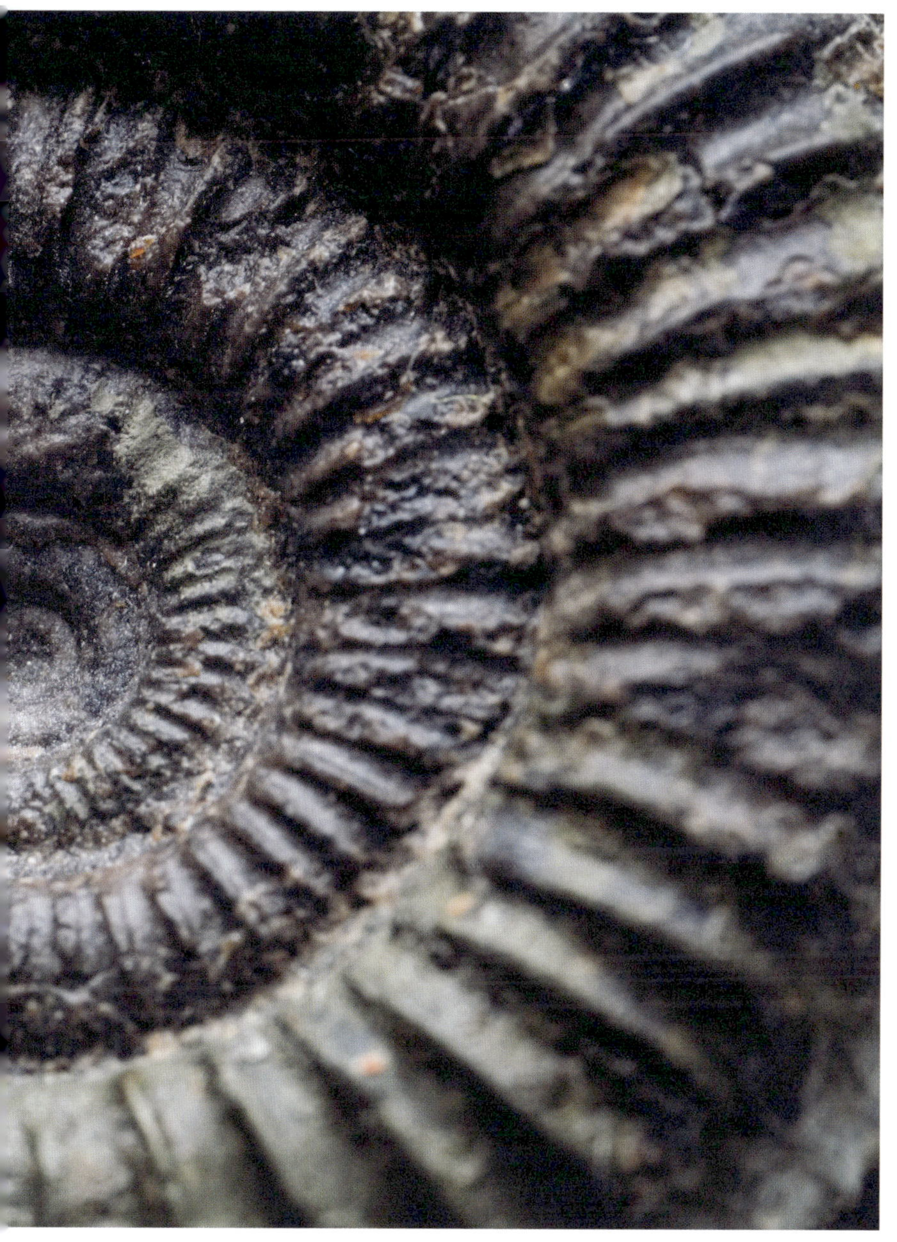

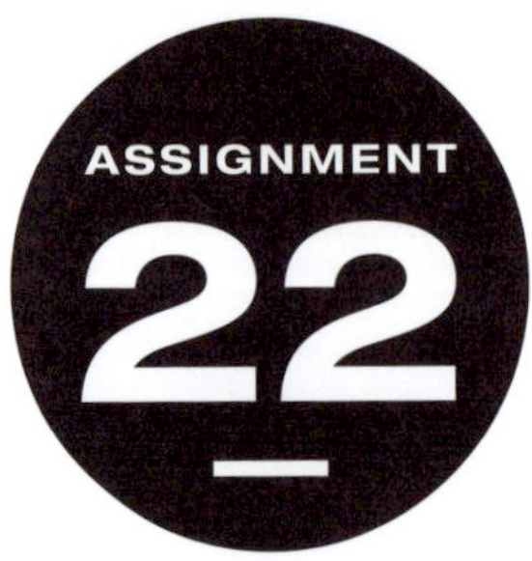

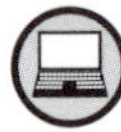

SPECIAL KIT

• Flatbed scanner

• Computer

• Black background

TIPS

• Clean the scanner glass with a lint-free cloth before you begin.

• Don't put anything too heavy on the glass.

• Use a sheet of glass placed over the subject to squash it down if necessary.

• To record a black background, leave the scanner lid open and either scan in a darkened room or cover the scanner with a large cardboard box.

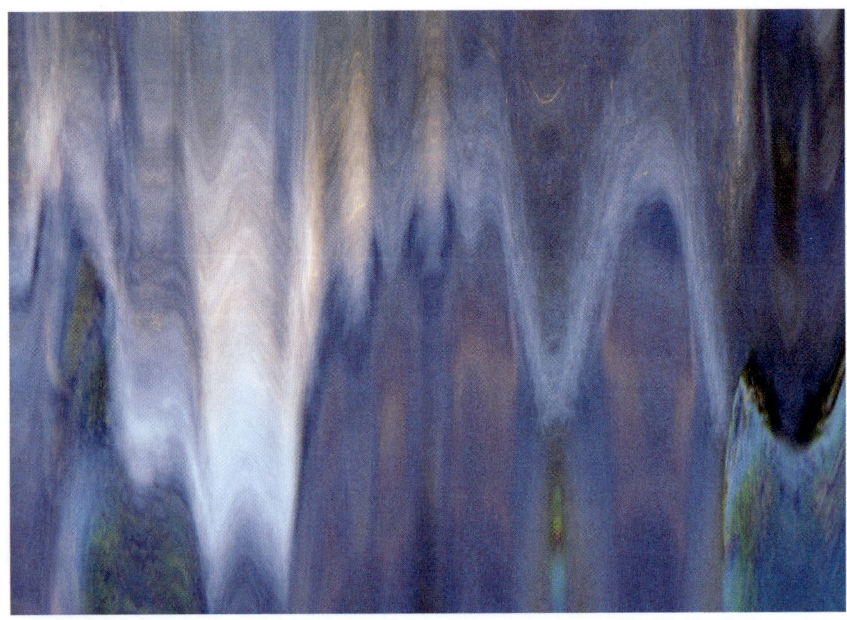

SCANOGRAPHY

Flatbed scanners are a fun way to create macro images without the need for a camera. The process is known as scanner photography, or scanography. Flatbed scanners with a built-in transparency hood—used to scan film negatives and slides—can also be used to scan translucent subjects (see assignment 42).

There are limitations to scanography, however. The first is that scanners are best suited to creating images of flat subjects. Depth-of-field is limited—typically between one to ten millimeters—as is the illumination from the scanning head; only the base of anything three-dimensional placed on the scanner glass will be sharp and correctly-exposed. Scanners are also slow and so the subject should ideally not move during the scan, although deliberate movement can be used to produce creative effects.

For this assignment, use a flatbed scanner to create a variety of images. Try using different subjects to see what works best with the technique, and experiment with a variety of backgrounds—such as different color tissue papers or leaving the lid open—to see what effect these have on the images.

◄ Scanning something takes a bit of time, and this can be used for effect. To create this image a print was moved during the scanning process, creating an abstract effect.

MACRO NOTES

How detailed the final image will be is dependent on the optical resolution of the scanner. This is measured in dots per inch (DPI) or dots per centimeter (DPCM). The higher the DPI/DPCM specification, the greater the detail resolved by the scanner. Selecting the highest DPI/DPCM setting will extend the scanning time but the resulting larger files will allow you more scope for cropping.

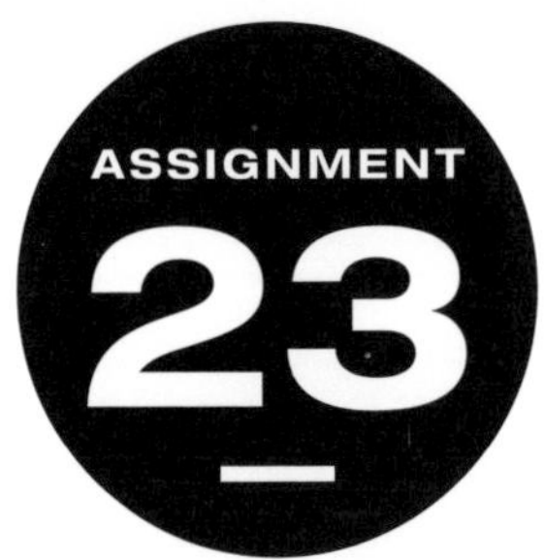

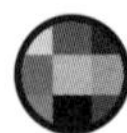

SPECIAL KIT

- Off-camera flash or lamp

- Tripod

- Clear glass dish or jug

TIPS

- Use the Hue slider in postproduction to shift the colors to suit.

- Magazine photos make colorful backgrounds.

- Use a dish that has minimal scratches if possible and clean it carefully before use.

SLICK TECHNIQUE

Oil and water don't mix: oil floats on the surface of water, creating interesting globular patterns. This makes the combination ideal for shooting abstract macro photos with a slightly unworldly visual quality that's very photogenic.

All you need is a clear dish, water, and a vegetable oil such as sunflower or olive oil. Mineral oil should not be used as it's more difficult to dispose of cleanly afterward. What oil and water aren't, however, is colorful. Color is added through the use of light colored by gels, or by using a colorful background below the dish.

Your brief for this assignment is to shoot a sequence of oil and water images. Select the best three and use postproduction to enhance color and contrast. Experiment with varying the lighting you use by altering its brightness and angle to the surface of the water. Don't be afraid to shoot lots of images as this will give you more choice later.

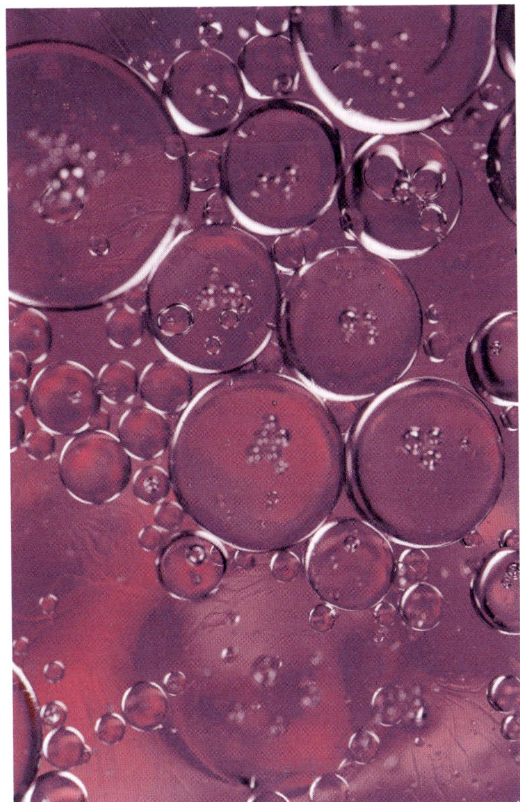

◀ *Adding a drop of liquid soap into the water will create more three-dimensional oil bubbles.*

MACRO NOTES

Flash sync speed is the fastest shutter speed that can be selected when shooting with flash. Typically sync speed is either 1/200 or 1/250 sec. Some flashes offer HSS shooting. This is High Speed Sync and lets you shoot flash using shutter speeds faster than the sync speed. The drawback is that the range of flash is often significantly reduced, although this is less of a problem when shooting macro imagery.

THE PROCESS

1 Add water to a dish or jug.

2 Mount your camera on a tripod so that the camera is above the dish or jug and pointing straight down.

3 Place the flash or lamp to the side of the dish or jug.

4 With the camera in Manual exposure mode, select a wide aperture to minimize depth-of-field.

5 Set the lens to manual focus and focus precisely on the surface of the water.

6 Set the shutter speed to 1/500 or 1/1000 sec (or the sync speed if using flash). Increase the ISO if necessary to avoid underexposure. Take a test shot to check exposure.

7 Select Continuous drive and then carefully pour the oil into the water, while keeping the bottle or jar out of shot. Fire the shutter as you do so.

8 Carefully agitate the surface of the water to break up the oil into new patterns and reshoot.

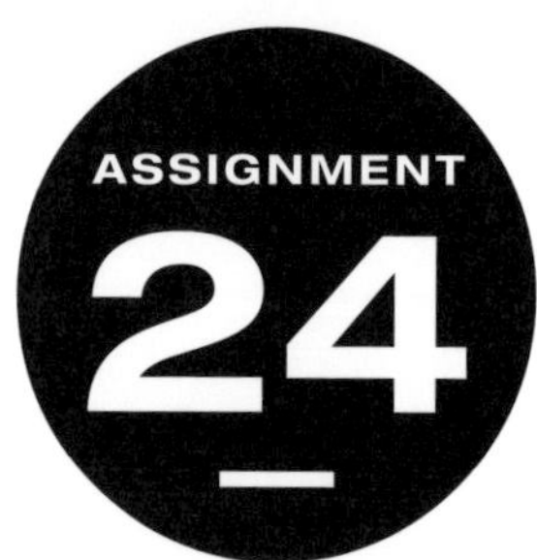

 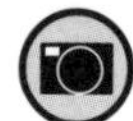
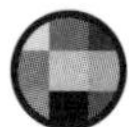 

SPECIAL KIT

- Flashlight
- Tripod

MACRO NOTES

Flashlights can be used as a direct light source for macro projects. Modern LED flashlights have a neutral-to-cool light similar to daylight. This can be easily colored through the use of gels or cellophane. Flashlights cast a hard light too that is easily softened by shining it through a diffuser, which could be as simple as a sheet of tissue paper. This will reduce the intensity of the light and so will require a longer exposure.

LIGHT TRAILS

Photography is usually simple. You look through the viewfinder and press the shutter button: what you see is what you get. However, this useful predictability is lost when using a long exposure to shoot a subject that moves. What's gained is a wonderfully random quality to your shots that can often never be repeated.

A light source that moves during an exposure will create a trail in the final image. This is often used to interesting effect when shooting flowing traffic at dusk. The effect can also be used in close-up and macro photography with a flashlight or other small point light source. How the light from the flashlight moves through the shot is entirely up to you and your imagination.

For this assignment, set up a still-life shot and use a flashlight to create light trails around the subject. Experiment with how fast or slow you move the flashlight, as well as how it moves through the exposure. Try circling the flashlight around the subject, for example, or using the flashlight to create an outline for the subject. Don't worry if initial results are disappointing. It can take time to get a feel for what works and what doesn't.

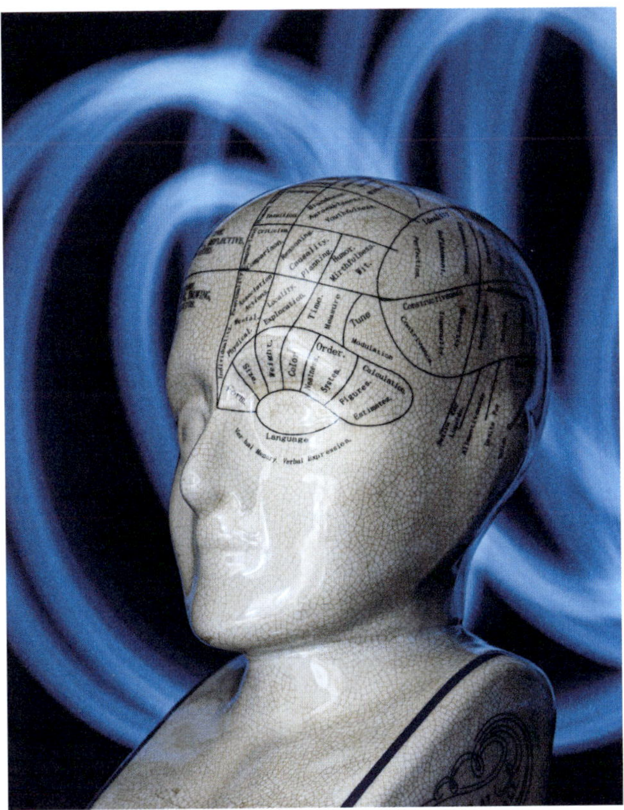

▲ *Smooth curves of light look more pleasing than jagged, random streaks, so keep your movement steady.*

THE PROCESS

1 Set up the subject on a flat surface in a room that can be easily darkened. Allow space so that you can move the flashlight around the subject without disturbing it.

2 Select Manual exposure mode and set the shutter speed to 15 or 30 seconds, the aperture to f/8, and an ISO value of between 100 and 400.

3 Switch the lens to manual focus and focus on your subject.

4 Select self-timer and a two-second delay. Turn your flashlight on.

5 Press the shutter button and, before the shutter fires, smoothly move the flashlight continuously around the subject until the exposure completes.

6 Review the shot and reshoot, varying the speed you move the flashlight or the length of time that the shutter is open, if necessary.

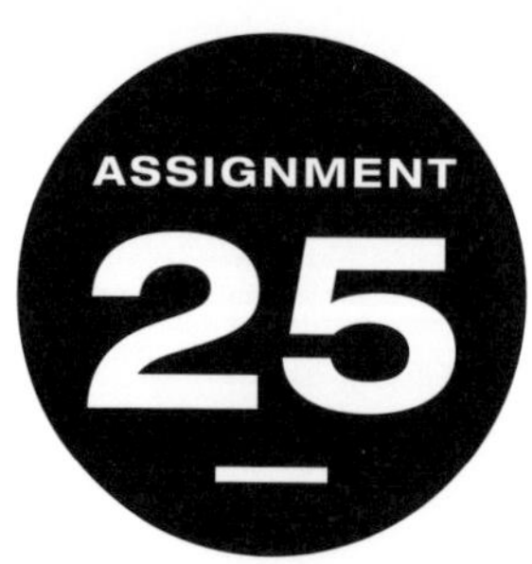

TIPS

- A macro lens with a long working distance will minimize the risk of frightening off an insect.

- Shoot at the same level as the insect for a more natural perspective.

- Buy a guidebook to insects to better understand where different species are likely to be found.

IT'S A BUG'S LIFE

Insects make rewarding and interesting macro subjects. There are a number of challenges that need to be overcome, however. The first is that insects are often lively and rarely stay in one place for long. They are also easily frightened off, unless great care is taken as you shoot.

Flying insects—such as dragonflies or butterflies—require external warmth to function. This warmth is typically derived from the sun, which means that these types of insects are often sluggish first thing in the morning and so easier to shoot. Insects that live in large colonies—such as ants or bees—are less dependent on the sun's heat and so they are active for longer during the day. A basic understanding of insect behavior is an important way to maximize your chance of success.

Your brief for this assignment is to shoot one particular insect species over the course of a week. Shoot a wide range of photos: as well as close-ups of your chosen insect, include images that show it in its natural environment or displaying different types of behavior.

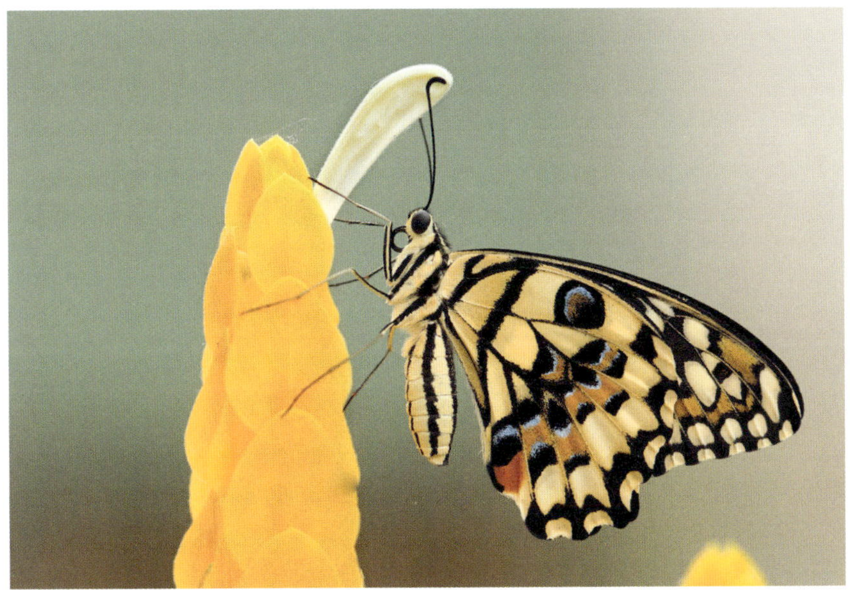

MACRO NOTES

Focus on the eyes of
the insect whenever
possible. We tend to
look at the eyes of a
subject first and it's
disturbing if these
are out-of-focus. Use
manual focus initially
and—if necessary—
gently move the
camera backward
or forward to refine
focus further.

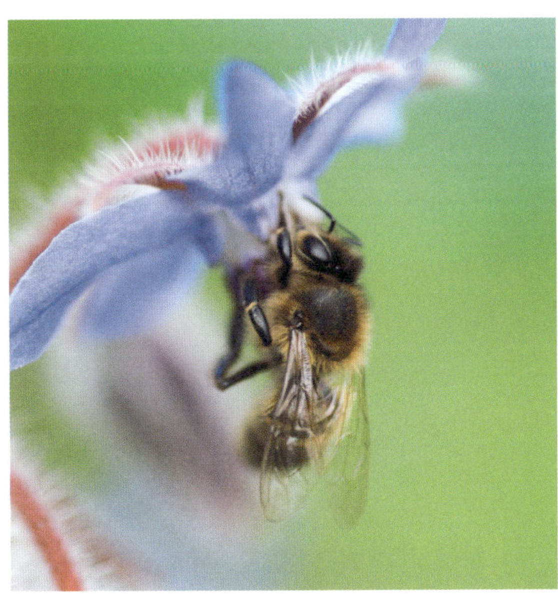

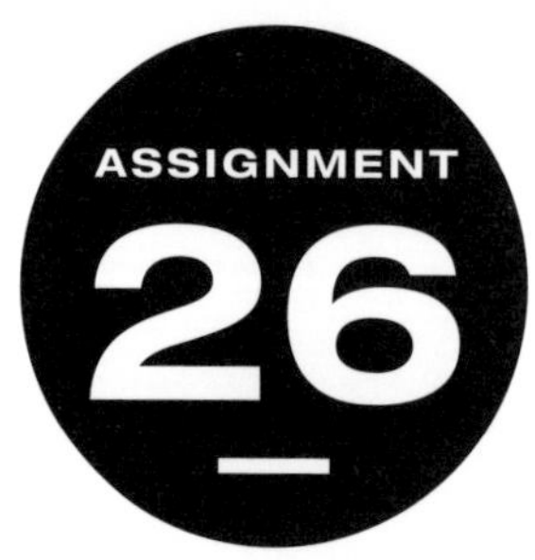

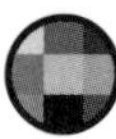

SPECIAL KIT

- Flowers

- Shallow dish or container

TIPS

- Use a container deep enough so that the flowers will be entirely encased in ice.

- The ice will begin to melt as soon as it's removed from the freezer, so have your photography equipment set up ready.

▶ *Backlighting, from a source such as a lightbox, works well as a lighting direction. Just be sure that it won't be affected by water as the ice melts!*

FROZEN BLOOMS

Artistic and colorful images can be made by shooting flowers frozen in water. Any flower will work, but there's something poignant and symbolic about flowers with romantic associations, such as roses, encased in ice.

Ordinary tap water contains impurities, such as minerals, that can turn the ice cloudy. Distilled water, made by condensing the steam from boiling water back into a liquid, is more likely to create clear ice. The flowers are best frozen in stages, with the ice gradually built up in layers. This can take some time so it's best to start the day before you plan to start shooting.

For this assignment, shoot flowers frozen in ice. Experiment with different varieties of flowers and the depth of ice (thicker ice will allow less light to pass through). Vary how you light the ice too, as well as how you compose your shots. This project will take some patience as ice does not last long once taken out of a freezer. Work on this assignment over the course of a week or two.

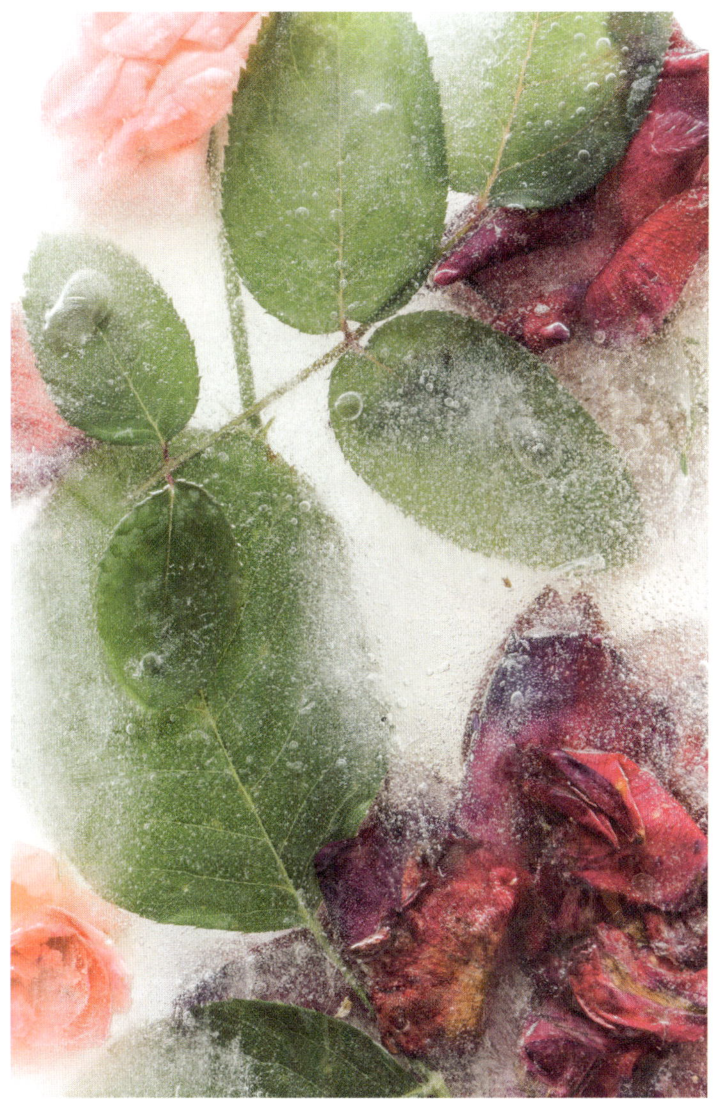

MACRO NOTES

Flowers aren't the only thing that can be frozen in ice. Imagination—and the size of your freezer—is the only limit on this technique. Other ways to vary your results include adding a food dye to the water to add color and using other liquids such as milk. However, don't use a liquid, container, or subject that it's unsafe or unwise to freeze.

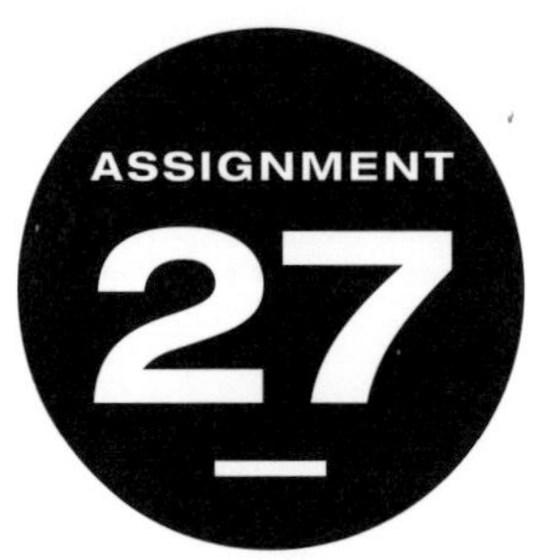

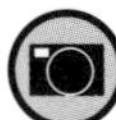

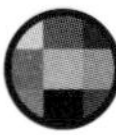

TIPS

- Direct light—such as the sun or from flash—will need to be diffused and softened.

- Bright tones can confuse your camera's exposure meter causing it to underexpose. Add one or two stops of positive exposure compensation to counteract this.

- Tweak brightness and contrast in postproduction if necessary.

HIGH-KEY

High-key is the term used to describe an image that's mainly made up of light tones with few mid or dark tones. It's a lighting technique that creates an open and airy feel, and is often used to convey carefree innocence in portraiture. High-key can also be used in macro; the challenge is to find a subject that suits the visual style. The benefit of shooting high-key is that it helps to simplify a shot and minimizes visual distractions.

The simplest way to shoot a high-key image is to overexpose the image. However, better results can be achieved by controlling the lighting. This involves illuminating the shadows so that they are reduced, either by using a reflector (see assignment 9) or with extra lighting. The background should also be well illuminated to the point where it's at least as brightly lit, if not brighter, than the subject.

Your brief is to shoot a high-key image. Think carefully about the subject and whether it would suit the high-key treatment. Experiment with lighting and exposure to see what produces the most pleasing effect.

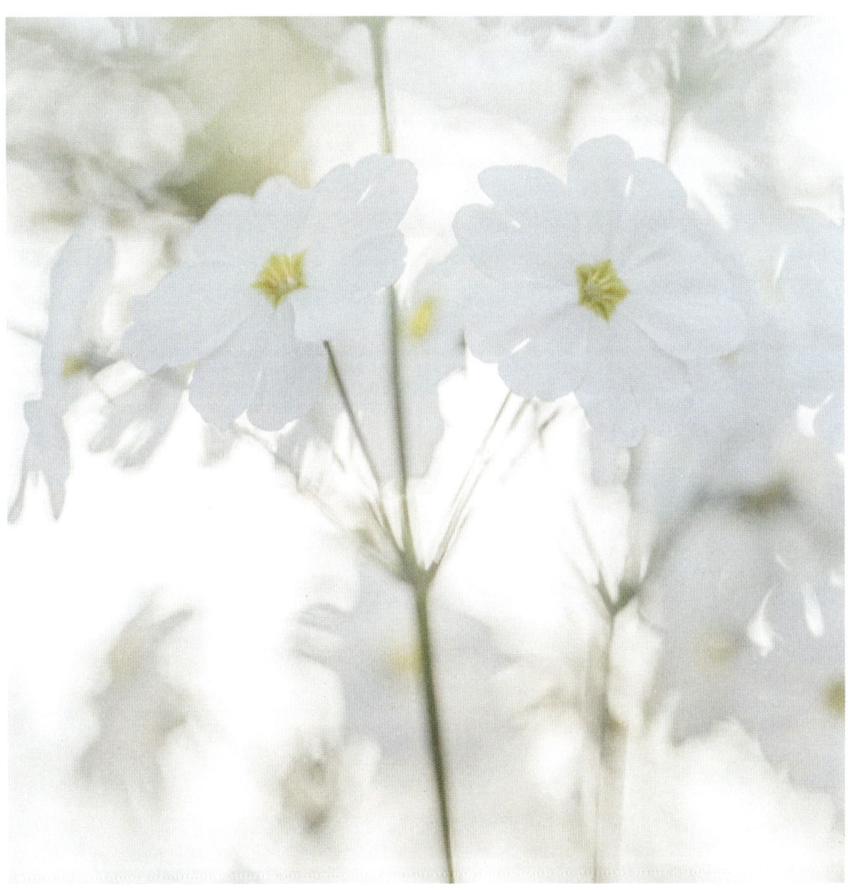

▲ *North-facing windows make excellent bright but evenly lit backgrounds for high-key subjects.*

MACRO NOTES

High-key lighting works best when two or more lights are used to illuminate the subject. The first is the key light and is the main source of illumination. The second light is the fill light, which is used to illuminate the shadows. The fill light should be less intense than the key light so that there are some shadows to define the shape of the subject.

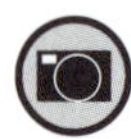

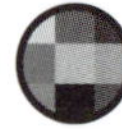

ASSIGNMENT

28

TIPS

- Any modification of flash will reduce the intensity of its output. TTL metering should take account of this but you may need to step in and adjust flash exposure compensation.

- Bouncing flash off a neutrally-colored surface onto your subject is another way of softening the light.

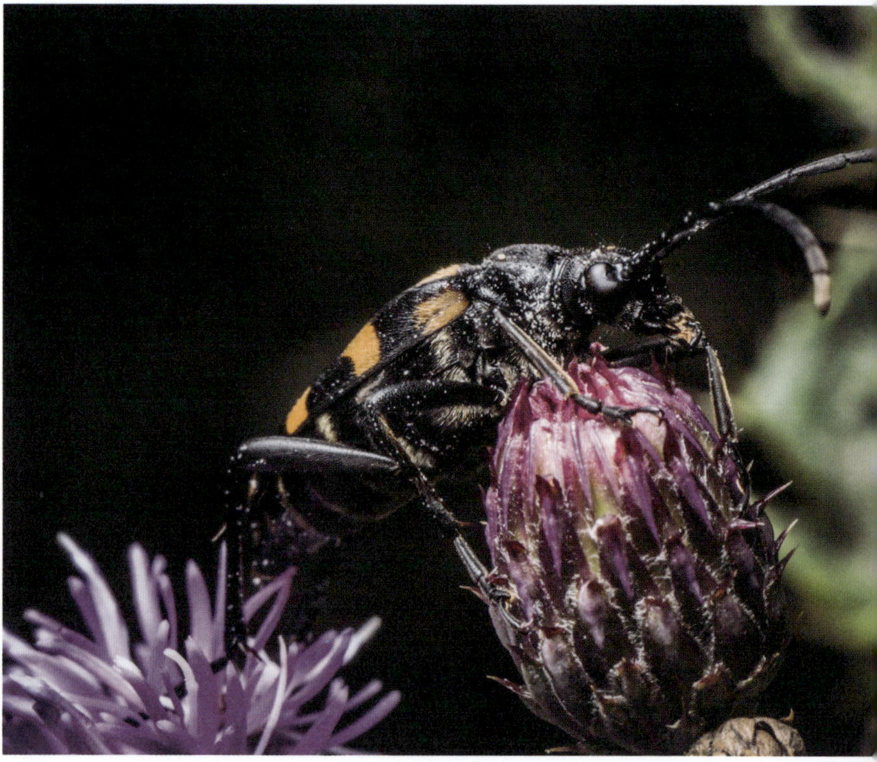

SOFTBOX AND DIFFUSERS

Flash is a wonderful tool for macro photography. Even the most basic flashgun is generally powerful enough to light close-up and macro subjects. However, flash is not perfect and there are limitations. One problem is that the light is hard and direct. Another is that the lens, when the flash is mounted on the camera, will cast a shadow over the subject.

The solution is to add a small softbox designed for use with flashguns, which will soften the light reaching the subject. Softboxes are readily available from most good camera stores. Ideally, a softbox should be roughly the length of your camera and macro lens combined, so that the front of the softbox is in line with the front of the lens.

Another way to soften flash light is to tape one end of a sheet of white paper to the flash head and the other to the front of the lens (without covering the front element of the lens). This is very effective at softening flash light without the expense of purchasing a softbox.

Experiment with flash diffusion for this assignment. Try using a piece of paper initially or look online for other ways to make DIY flash diffusers. Ultimately a softbox is a more permanent solution and something to consider for later.

◀ *A softbox creates soft and attractive highlights on shiny surfaces, such as the body and eyes of insects.*

MACRO NOTES

TTL stands for Through The Lens and is generally the default option for flash exposure. TTL puts the camera in charge of flash exposure and is generally very accurate and consistent, though not infallible. Flash exposure compensation allows you to adjust flash exposure either via an option on the camera's menu system or on the flashgun itself.

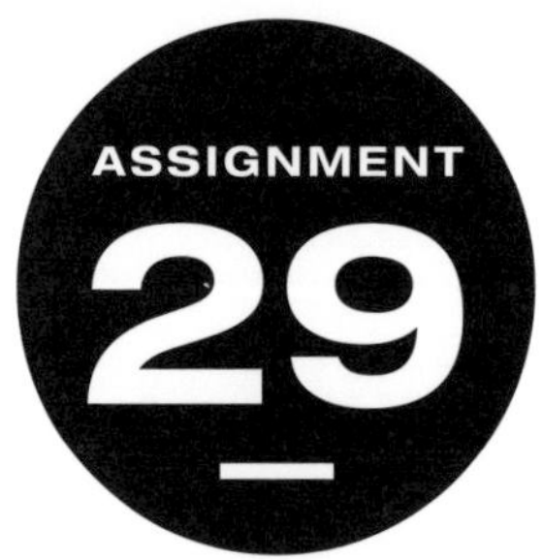

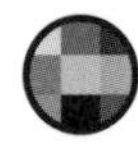

- Tripod

- Reflector

- Mirror

- Gently clean leaf litter away from the fungi to simplify the shots.

- Fungi grow and then decay rapidly and so it's worth returning to a potentially favorable location on a daily basis over the course of a week.

FUNGI

Fungi in their many and varied forms can usually be found all year round. However, they are more common in the misty and damp months of fall, particularly in deciduous woodland. Fungi are not plants but in a kingdom all their own. They don't photosynthesize, but instead extract the nutrients they need from food sources such as rotting wood.

The most recognizable type of fungi are capped mushrooms and toadstools. These often feature intricate and photogenic gill structures below the cap. Unfortunately, mushrooms often grow close to the ground and so shooting low down is usually necessary. Reflectors are a simple way to bounce light up into the cap. Mirrors with a silvered surface are also useful tools that—by shooting the reflection—make creating images of the underside of mushrooms far easier. Other types of fungi include bracket fungus, that grow out like shelving from trees, and lichens, which are a symbiotic composite of algae and fungi, and are usually found growing on stone and other flat surfaces. All have close-up and macro photographic potential.

Your brief for this assignment is to find and shoot a variety of fungi. Use guidebooks or the Internet to help you discover where and when they might be found locally. Try a range of different approaches to the subject, including shooting the fungi in context as well as more detailed images of the subject's structure. Use store-bought mushrooms if wild fungi are hard to find.

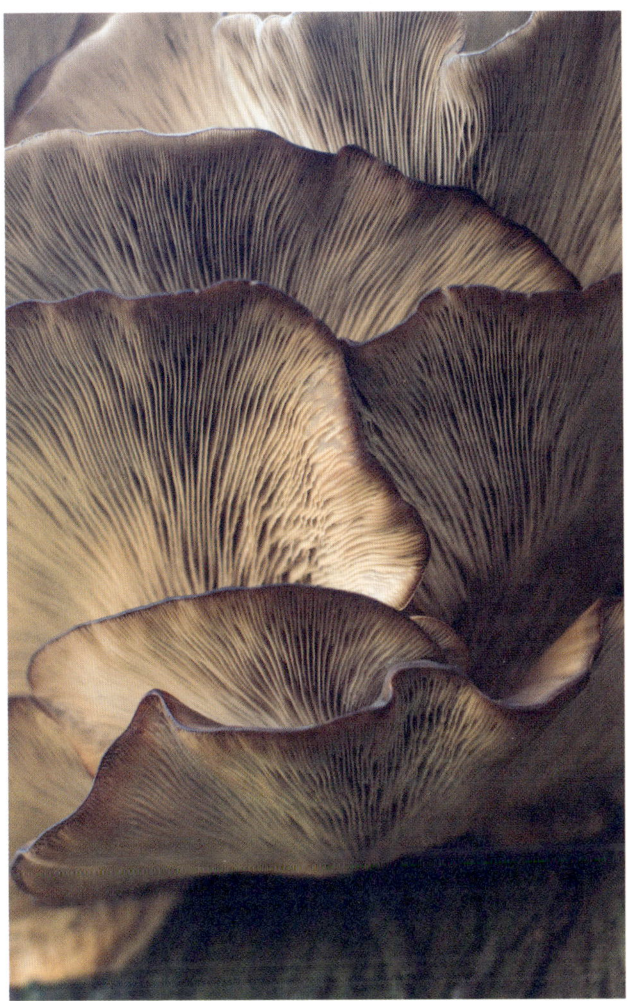

▲ *The most interesting details of fungi are often underneath, where the lamella (gills) are usually found.*

MACRO NOTES

A standard mirror is made from a sheet of glass with silvering added to the back of the glass. This can cause a distracting double reflection when used for photography. Mirrors with the reflective coating on the surface of the glass are more expensive and prone to scratching, but invaluable for shooting underneath low subjects.

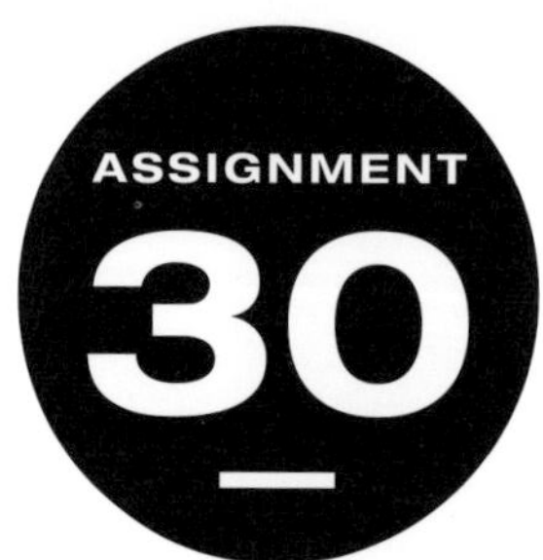

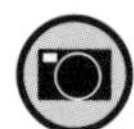
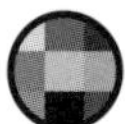

SPECIAL KIT

- Tripod
- Off-camera flash
- Softbox
- Sheet of white card

TIPS

- If depth-of-field is an issue, focus precisely on the most important part of the jewelry, such as a precious stone or engraving.
- Clean up blemishes such as scratches in postproduction unless they can be removed before shooting.
- Use the Flash White Balance preset for accurate color reproduction.

JEWELRY

Jewelry is often small and delicate, making it ideal as a macro photography subject. The main challenge with jewelry is that it's often also shiny and highly reflective. This means that care needs to be taken not only with how jewelry is lit, but also where you place the camera and any other necessary equipment.

Flash is a point light source and—if used on its own—will create distracting bright highlights on jewelry. Light from a flash can be softened by fitting a softbox to the flash. Ideally, the softbox should be big enough so that it doesn't cause distracting highlights. The smaller the softbox, the closer it will need to be to the jewelry to avoid this. Your camera equipment may also create distracting reflections. These can be reduced by shooting through a hole in a large piece of card held in front of the camera. (Use white card and this too will act as a reflector to soften the light.)

For this assignment shoot pieces of jewelry. Think about the background and how it can be used to enhance the shots. Consider using relevant props to create a story, such as a rose placed near a wedding ring, and experiment with lighting to see how this affects the final images.

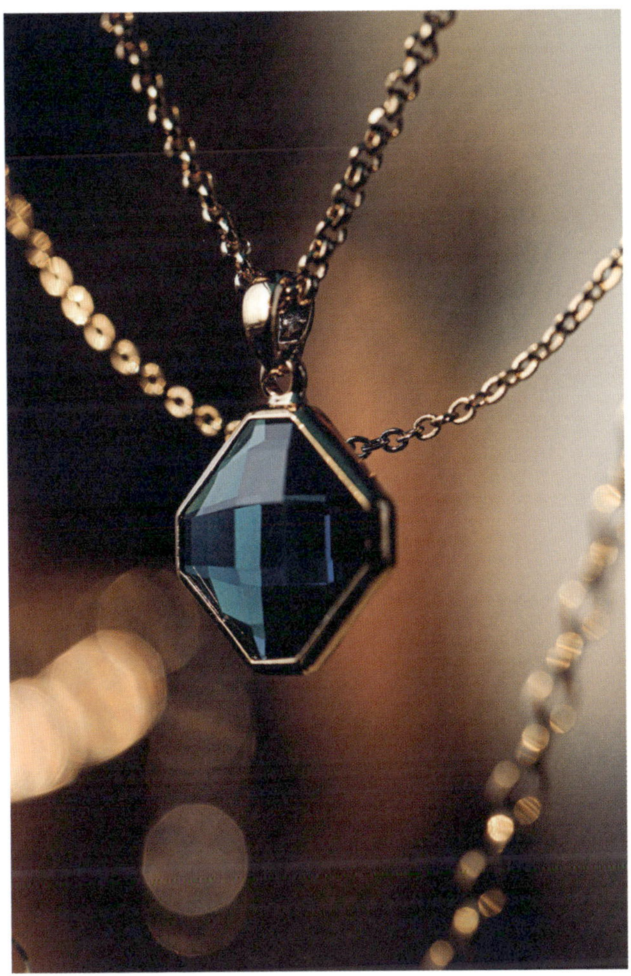

▲ *A simple background will be less distracting.*

MACRO NOTES

Off-camera flash can be triggered a number of different ways. The simplest way is with a sync cable connecting the flash to the camera. Wireless systems are a more convenient option as they allow you to freely move your flash around, as well as avoiding mishaps by accidentally pulling the cable. This requires a flash capable of being triggered wirelessly either by a slave flash or radio transmitter fitted to the hotshoe of the camera.

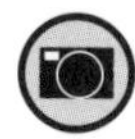

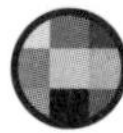

SPECIAL KIT

- Ring light

TIPS

- Ring lights are designed to wrap around a lens, but they can also be used off-camera too. There's no reason not to use them to provide other types of lighting, such as side lighting.

- Use a fast shutter speed to underexpose the background and make your subject stand out more.

RINGING AROUND

The working distance of a lens is a measurement of the space between the front element of the lens and the subject of the photo. When shooting macro, the working distance is often very short, sometimes as little as a few centimeters or less. With such a short working distance, it can be a problem to light the subject effectively, which may even be in the shadow of the camera.

A ring light solves this problem. This is a circular shaped light that screws to the filter thread of a lens. This provides a soft but bright light that evenly illuminates the subject. One downside to ring lights is that they create very distinctive round specular highlights, particularly when shooting glossy or reflective subjects.

For this assignment use a ring light to shoot a set of photos. Select a wide range of subjects, each with a different texture, color, and shape. See what type of subject best suits the use of a ring light and what does not. Experiment with exposure too, altering the power output of the ring light to see how this affects the illumination at different distances.

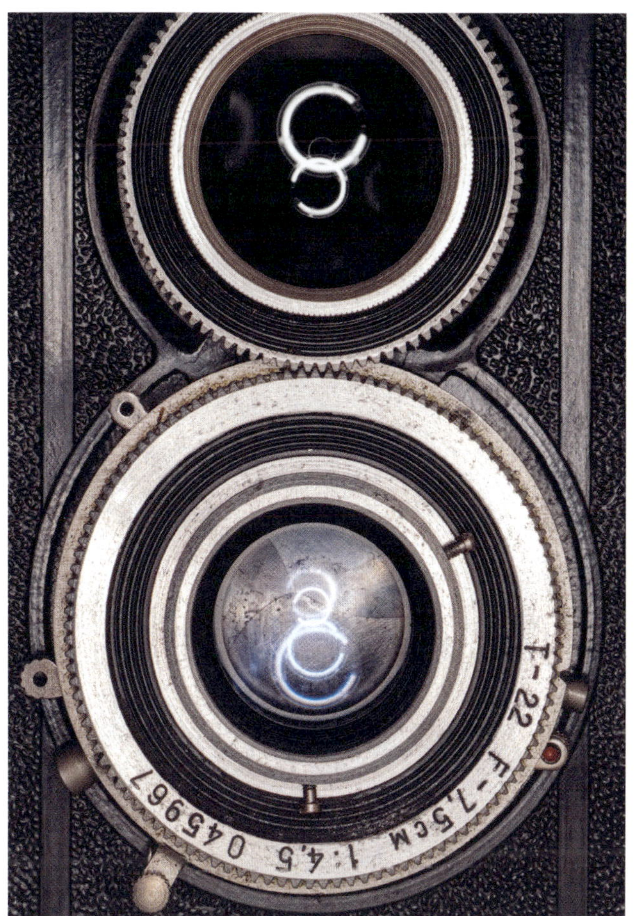

▲ *The bright, round reflections created by ring lights can be very attractive with the right subject.*

MACRO NOTES

Ring lights come in two forms: flash or LED. Flash ring lights are typically the more powerful of the two and are attached by a wired connection to the camera's hotshoe. LED ring lights are easier to use as the light is constant so you can see the effect before you shoot. Some ring lights allow you to switch off one half of the ring to create shadows on one side of your subject for a more three-dimensional effect.

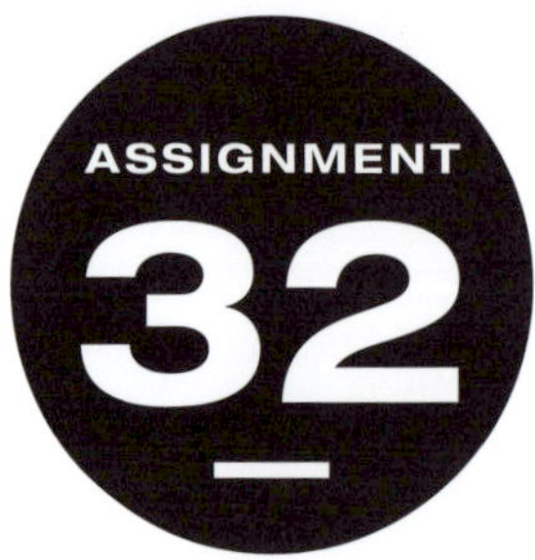

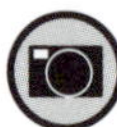

SPECIAL KIT

- Tripod

- Light source

- Coins and banknotes

TIPS

- Copper coins are less reflective than silver coins and are easier to light evenly.

- Use a dark background or one that isn't visually distracting.

▼ *Two colored light sources were used to add visual interest to this image of a coin.*

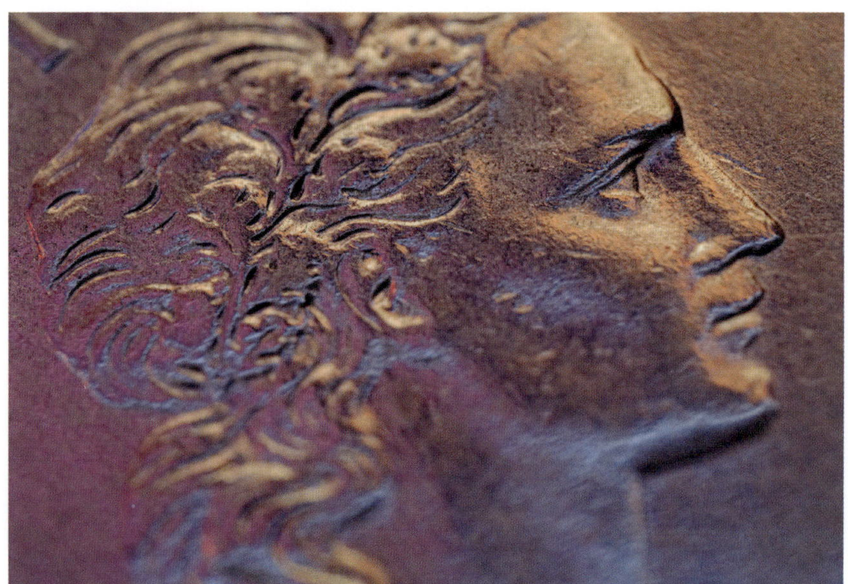

COINS AND BANKNOTES

Coins and banknotes are deliberately designed with fine detail in order to make forgery more difficult. These details are photogenic and so coins and banknotes make good macro subjects. What's particularly fascinating is the way that currency gradually wears through use. Older coins become scratched and tarnished, while banknotes become creased and torn. The first aesthetic choice you're faced with is therefore old or new? Old coins are easy to find but new, freshly minted coins will need to be acquired directly from either a bank or currency dealer.

Another aesthetic choice is how coins, in particular, are lit. The most common way to light coins is to use a large, soft light source, either from a lightbox or softbox. This shadowless light minimizes bright highlights but isn't particularly exciting. More interesting effects can be created by using a sidelight, which helps to reveal the detail and texture of the coins. This lighting is inherently contrasty, but this effect can be reduced by the use of a reflector (see assignment 9).

Your assignment is to shoot a variety of coins and banknotes. Vary the approach you take as you shoot, changing how you light and compose the shots. Start with a flat light and a straight-on composition and go from there.

ASSIGNMENT JOURNAL

MACRO NOTES

Copy or repro stands are often used to photograph subjects such as coins. These are stands mounted to a board. When mounted to the stand, a camera can be moved very precisely and consistently up and down relative to the board. Some copy stands have built-in lights that provide flat and even illumination across subjects placed on the board.

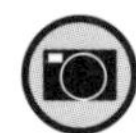
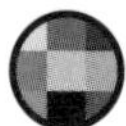

SPECIAL KIT

- Tripod
- Black background
- Desk lamp or off-camera flash
- Snoot
- Reflector (optional)

TIPS

- Use a telephoto lens to keep your camera from being affected by heat and any particles from the smoke.
- Ventilate the room every ten minutes and once you've finished shooting.
- Shoot in Raw for greater flexibility with exposure correction in postproduction.

UP IN SMOKE

Shooting smoke successfully requires preplanning and careful setting up. However, with practice, the resulting images will have an enchanting ethereal quality unlike any other subject.

Incense sticks are ideal for shooting smoke images as they burn gradually allowing you time to shoot, and shouldn't set off any nearby smoke detectors either. Candles shouldn't produce smoke so they're not suitable for this assignment. To make the smoke stand out, the incense stick should be shot against a black background and side lit by a light or flash fitted with a snoot.

Your brief for this assignment is to shoot a selection of smoke images. Experiment to see what effects you can create. Smoke is affected by air currents so you need to shoot in a breeze-free environment. However, you can alter the shapes produced by the smoke by gently blowing across its path. Adding a gel to your flash or light will affect the color of the smoke, as will selecting different White Balance presets.

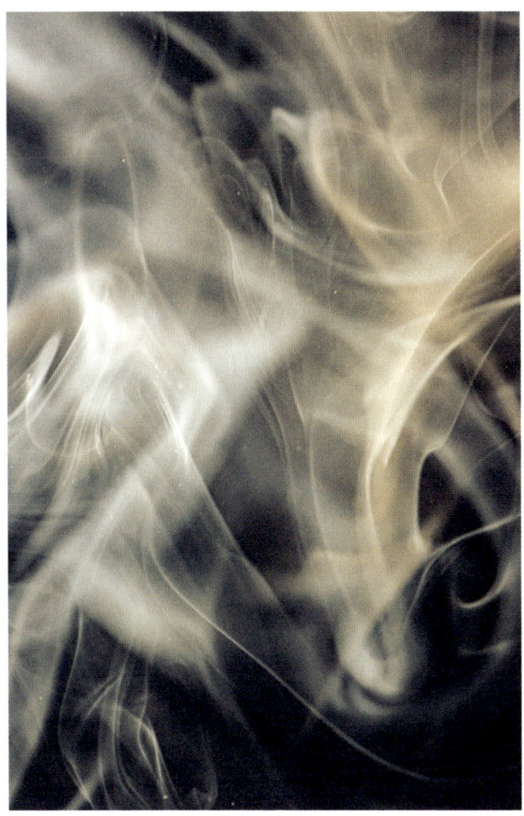

MACRO NOTES

A snoot is essentially just a hollow tube fitted to a light source and is used to direct light in only one particular direction. This prevents light spill into areas of the scene that should either remain dark or are being illuminated another way. Commercial snoots are available for studio lights and flashes. However, the same effect can be achieved by using a cardboard tube or pieces of card fitted around the head of a light or flash.

THE PROCESS

1 Place the incense stick approximately one meter in front of a black backdrop.

2 Place your light source—fitted with a snoot—to the side of and pointing toward the incense stick. Place the reflector on the other side of the incense stick to the light source.

3 Light the incense stick.

4 Compose the shot with the camera mounted on a tripod.

5 Focus on the stream of smoke using manual focus.

6 With the camera set to Manual exposure mode, select a low ISO rating, a shutter speed of 1/250 sec, and a mid-range aperture such as f/8 or f/11.

7 Take a test shot and adjust exposure if necessary.

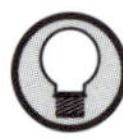

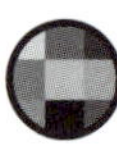

────── ──────

TIPS

- Use directional light to reveal differences in texture and shape, and softer light for color contrast.

- Contrast can also be conceptual: old versus new or natural versus artificial.

──────

▼ *The contrast here is between the softness of the feather and the hardness of the metal surface below.*

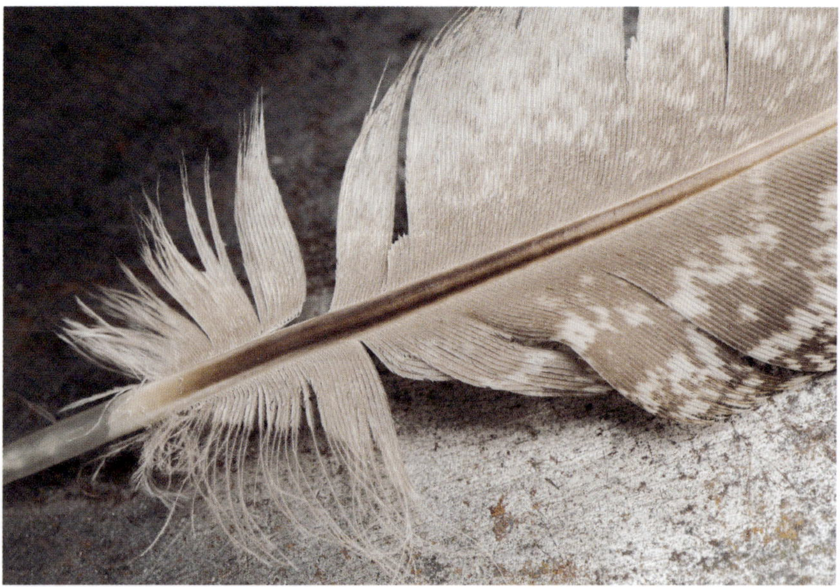

MIXING IT UP

In photography, contrast is usually thought of as purely the difference in brightness between the darkest area of any image and the lightest. However, there is also visual contrast, where two elements in the image noticeably differ in some way. This can be in terms of texture: hard or soft, rough or smooth, shiny or matte. Contrast can also take the form of a difference in shape: rounded or sharp-edged, simple or complex, fuzzy or solid. Color can also create contrast: color can be dull or saturated, warm or cool, dark or pastel.

Juxtaposing elements that are visually different adds interest to an image. Examples can be found in nature or an urban environment, but often it's simpler to create the juxtaposition yourself. For this assignment, find or bring together and shoot two elements that have visual contrast. Maximize this contrast so the differences between the elements are readily apparent. Repeat the exercise to create a portfolio of images.

MACRO NOTES

Complementary colors are those found on the opposite side of a color wheel. Orange and blue are commonly used to complement each other in design and photography, as are green and magenta. Although complementary colors are visually very different, they are pleasing when combined. Warmer colors are more visually "heavy" than cooler colors. For this reason, you would typically favor the cool color in terms of how much space it occupies in the image space.

ASSIGNMENT JOURNAL

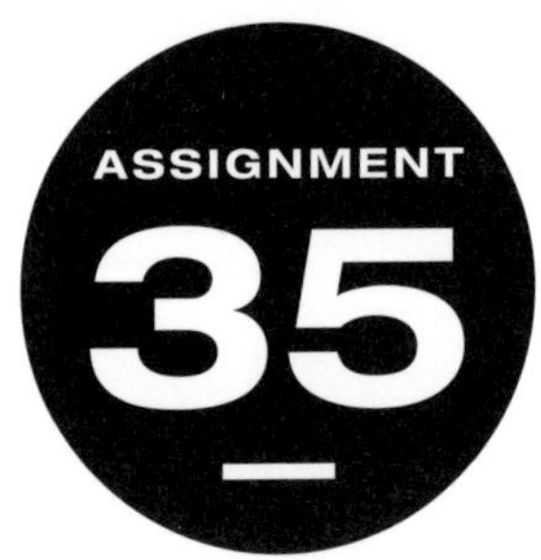

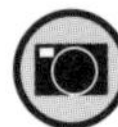
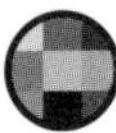

SPECIAL KIT

- Tripod

- Light source such as flash, a desktop lamp, or studio lighting

TIPS

- Check your histogram and tweak exposure if necessary.

- Use postproduction to darken shadows further.

LOW-KEY

Low-key images are those that are largely made up of dark tones with very few mid or light tones. (The exact opposite of high-key—see assignment 27.) Low-key lighting can be used to create moody, atmospheric images that convey dark emotions such as fear or sadness. As with high-key, low-key lighting can also be used when shooting macro if a suitable subject is available.

Creating successful and pleasing low-key images requires controlling how light falls on your subject and its immediate surroundings. The simplest way to do this is to use a single point light source, such as flash or a studio light. Barn doors fitted to the light will prevent unwanted light spilling onto the background, which should be darker than the subject. (Using black paper or cloth as a background will also help enormously.) Using back or side lighting is preferable as this will illuminate a more limited area of the subject.

Your brief is to select three things about your home and shoot them in a low-key manner. Choose objects that have an interesting shape or form and that would suit the low-key approach.

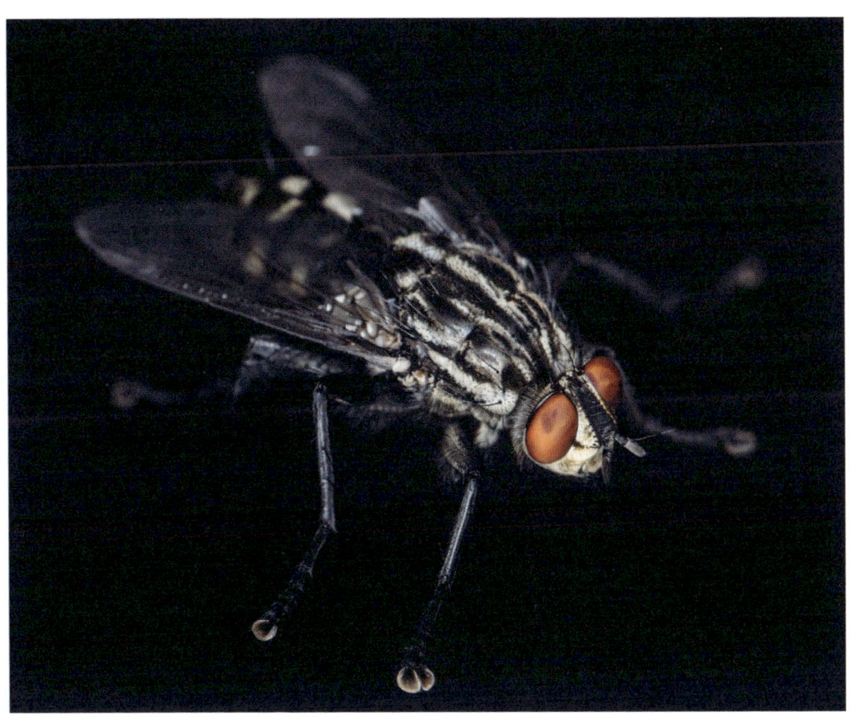

ASSIGNMENT JOURNAL

MACRO NOTES

A barn door is an accessory that can be fitted to flash or studio lighting. There are four hinged flaps on a barn door that can be individually positioned to direct how light falls on a scene. The effect can be replicated by using pieces of card held or taped close to the light source.

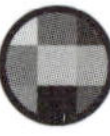

TIPS

- Colors convey emotion. Warm colors, such as red and yellow, are more likely to evoke positive emotions compared to a cool color, such as blue.

- The background should be in the same tonal range as your subject.

▼ *Green, yellow, and orange are analogous colors and are commonly found combined in natural subjects.*

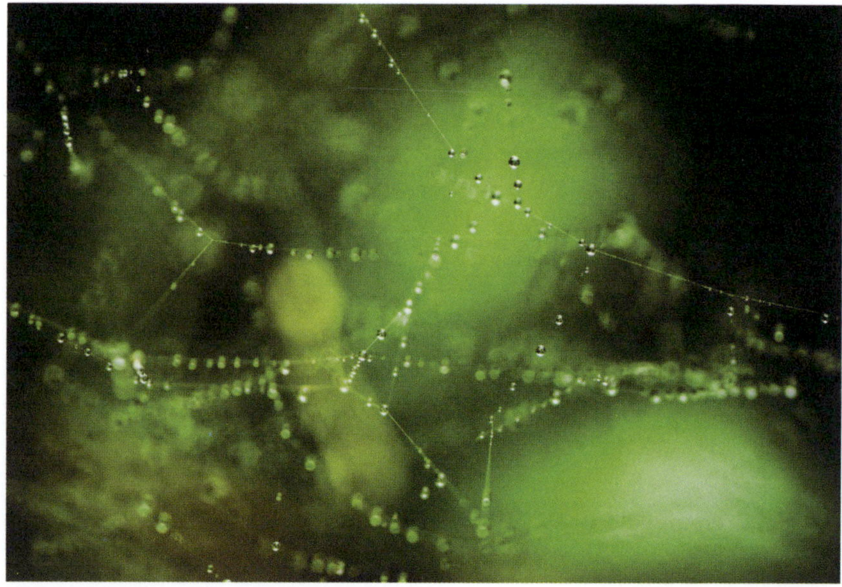

LIMITING COLOR RANGE

An analogous color harmony is one consisting of three colors that are adjacent on a color wheel. Using the limited palette of an analogous color harmony will create a pleasing restful image, particularly when using cooler colors such as blues and greens. The colors in an analogous color harmony can be vibrant or subdued, the key is excluding any color that clashes or would be a visual distraction.

In many ways, shooting an analogous color harmony image is similar to shooting in black and white. The limited color range will force you to think more about the shapes and textures within the scene and how they are arranged within your composition. Nature is a good place to look for analogous color harmonies, such as the golds and browns of fall or the vibrant greens and yellows of spring. Light can be used to create analogous color harmonies. By adding a gel to flash or studio lighting, objects—particularly reflective materials such as metal—will take on the color of the light source.

Your assignment is to shoot a series of analogous color harmony images. Use a color wheel to help you to choose the right colors.

MACRO NOTES

Color Temperature Orange (CTO) gels add warmth to flash light. They are typically used when you want to match the color temperature of flash to the warm artificial lighting. Color Temperature Blue (CTB) gels cool flash light down so that it matches overcast, dusk, or shade light.

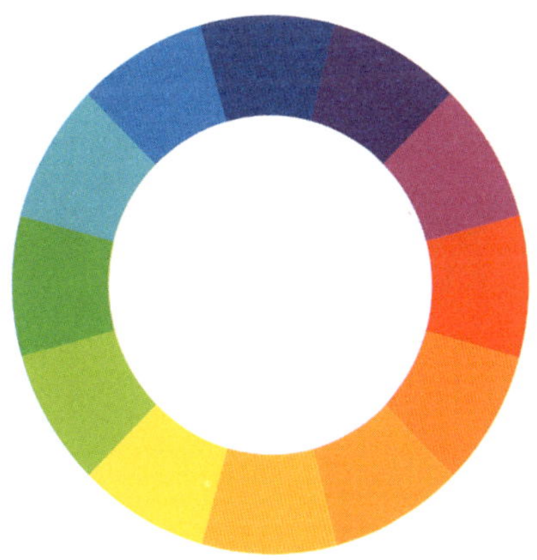

◄ *Use any three adjacent colors on a color wheel to create an analogous harmony.*

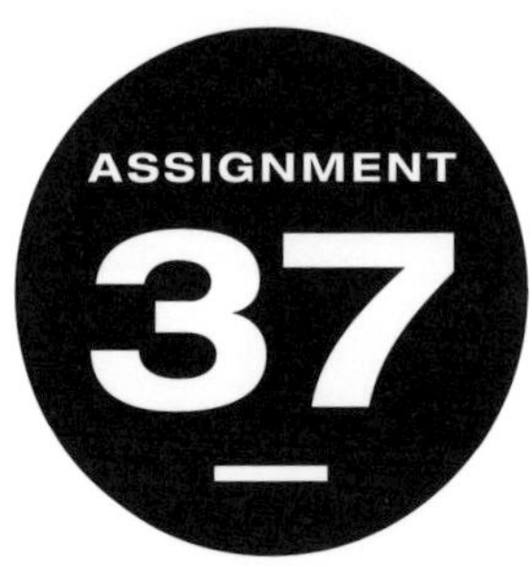

ASSIGNMENT
37

 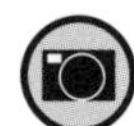
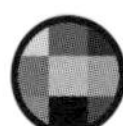 

SPECIAL KIT

• Tripod

TIPS

• Hard lighting (see assignment 16) will create interesting shadows.

• Side lighting will reveal form and texture.

ASSIGNMENT JOURNAL

▶ *A string of Christmas lights provided the illumination for this shot. A shallow depth-of-field ensured that they were out-of-focus and unrecognizable.*

MACRO NOTES

Selecting the "wrong" White Balance preset is a simple way to shift the color values of an image in an interesting way. Shooting using natural light but selecting a Tungsten or Fluorescent preset will add a cool blue cast to a shot, for example.

COMPLETING THE CIRCUIT

The insides of old and unwanted computer equipment offer a wide variety of subjects for macro photography. PC motherboards are usually complex, a maze of wires, components, and circuits. The platters of hard drives—once the casing has been removed—are wonderfully reflective and are perfect for lighting in interesting ways. However, the first task before starting—after unplugging the computer!—is giving everything a good clean with a blower or brush. Electronics attract dust, so the insides of PCs are rarely clean.

There is a huge number of ways to shoot your chosen subjects. Circuit boards have patterns that can be shot in an abstract way. Vertical components clustered together can resemble miniature cityscapes, with the circuit tracks taking on the form of roads. Orange-colored lighting can add to the effect by suggesting sunrise or sunset. Depth-of-field can be used creatively too. A shallow depth-of-field—when shooting the circuitry at an angle—can be used to emphasize particular aspects of the motherboard, for example.

Your assignment is to shoot ten images using the motherboard and peripherals of obsolete computer equipment (or any electronic device you may have to hand). Make each image different, varying the lighting and how you compose the shots.

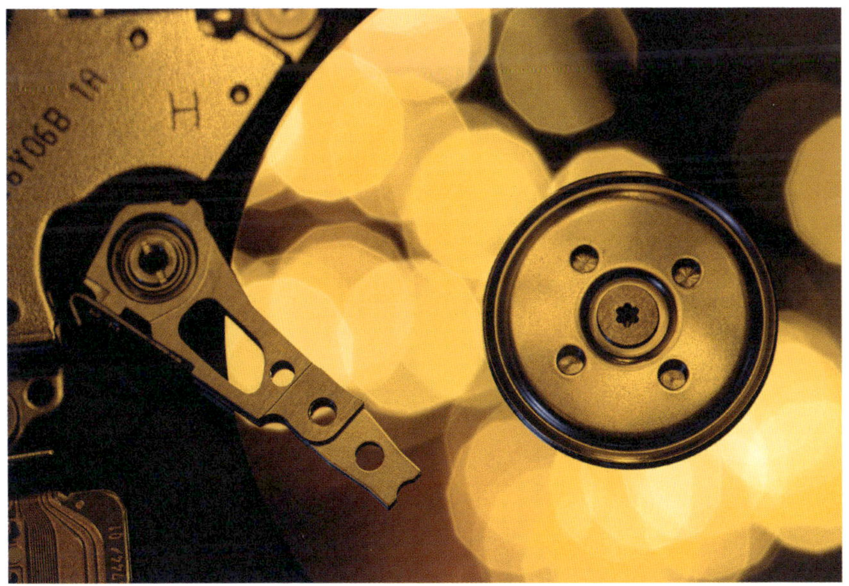

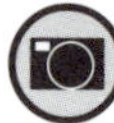

SPECIAL KIT

- Tripod

- Studio light or ring light

TIPS

- LED ring lights provide a usefully consistent illumination when shooting video.

- Move your camera slowly and smoothly when recording to avoid jerky footage.

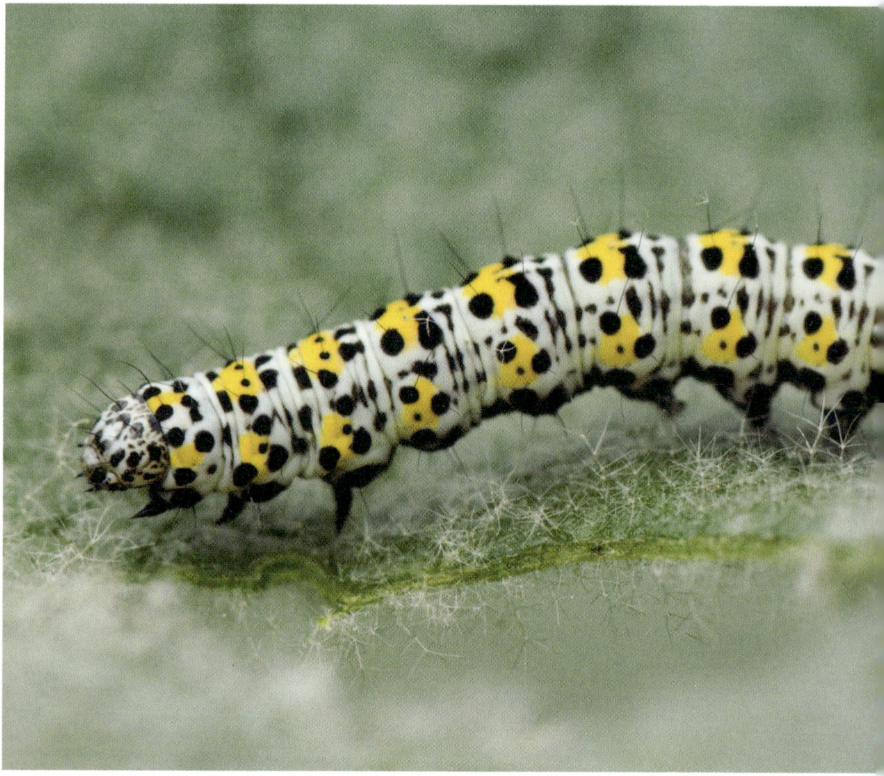

MACRO MOVIES

A camera's video mode is just as capable of shooting macro footage as any other subject. The key to creating interesting macro video is through movement. This can be achieved either by moving the camera as you shoot or by picking a subject that moves, such as insects like bees or ants.

Exposure options are more limited when shooting video than stills, however. Generally, the shutter speed should be twice that of the selected video frame rate (a convention known as the 180° shutter rule). This creates smooth-looking footage that looks natural. Slower shutter speeds can cause movement to look smeared, whereas faster shutter speeds can create footage with an over-sharp look that can be tiring to watch. Shooting macro footage often means selecting high ISO ratings, or using strong continuous lighting to illuminate a scene. (Using a wide aperture is another option, but depth-of-field will then be compromised.)

Keeping your subject in focus can be a challenge too, particularly if its movement is erratic. Using subtle manual adjustments is preferable to relying on autofocus, which can struggle when shooting video, particularly in low light. For this assignment shoot a macro movie. If you have the facility to edit clips together, consider creating a sequence using shots from different angles or with different subjects.

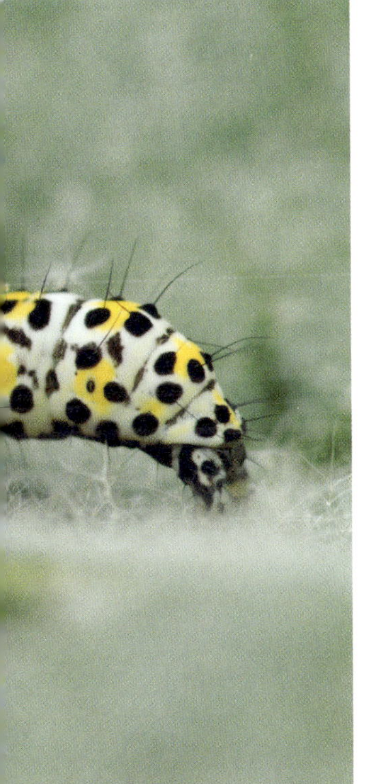

MACRO NOTES

There may be times when the shutter speed is too high, even when a low ISO rating and a small aperture are selected. The solution is to fit a Neutral Density (ND) filter to the lens. This reduces the amount of light hitting the sensor and so allows the use of slower shutter speeds. Variable ND filters are ideal for movie work as the amount of filtration can be varied. This is particularly useful if light levels change as you record.

◀ *The 16:9 aspect ratio of video is far narrower than the 3:2 or 4:3 default shape of a still photograph. This shape suits horizontal movement across the frame more than vertical movement.*

 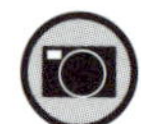 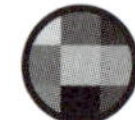

 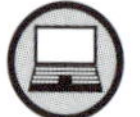

SPECIAL KIT

- Tripod

- Focusing rail

- Remote release

TIPS

- Turn on LCD/EVF frame guidelines as these will be a useful guide to how an image could be cropped later. They are also useful as a guide when shooting a series of images for stitching.

- Stitching can be combined with the stacking technique (see assignment 49) for ultra-sharp panoramics.

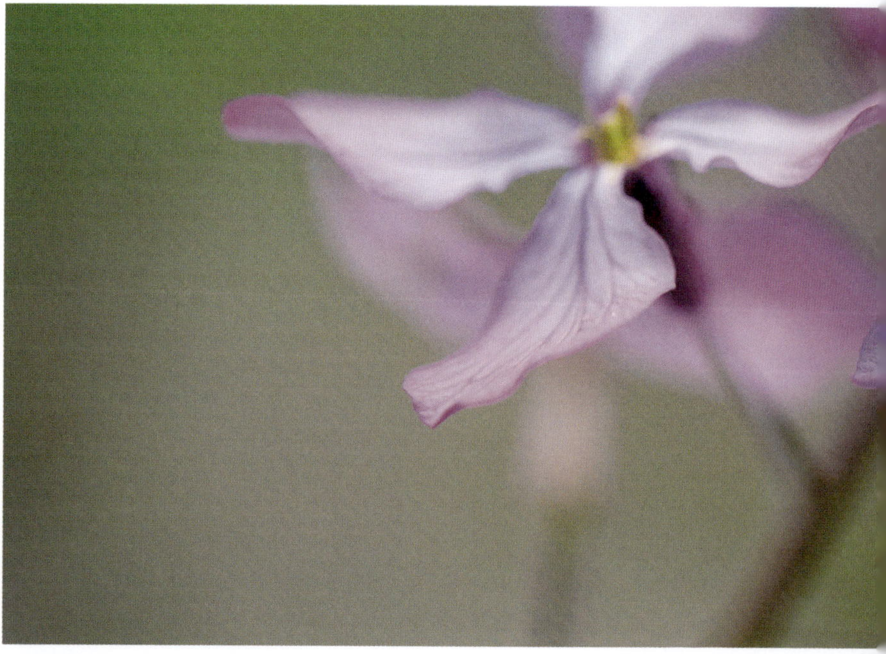

PANORAMA

When one dimension of an image is at least twice as long as the other, then that image is said to be panoramic. Usually panoramic images are shot horizontally, but it is not a rule to follow blindly; tall panoramics are strikingly unusual and eye-catching.

Panoramics are often used to convey the scope of a wide-open landscape, but there's no reason why the technique can't be used for macro photography too. The key is either choosing the right subject—one that would fit neatly into the letterbox shape of a panoramic—or by creating a composition that has a number of interesting elements that lead the eye across the frame.

▼ *Use the shape of your subject as an indicator of a suitable orientation for your panoramic image.*

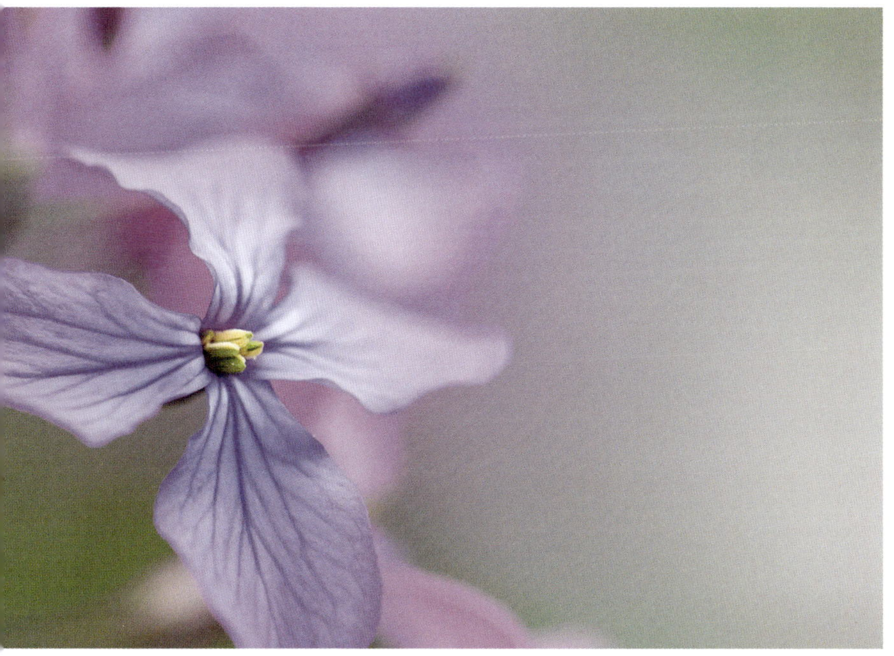

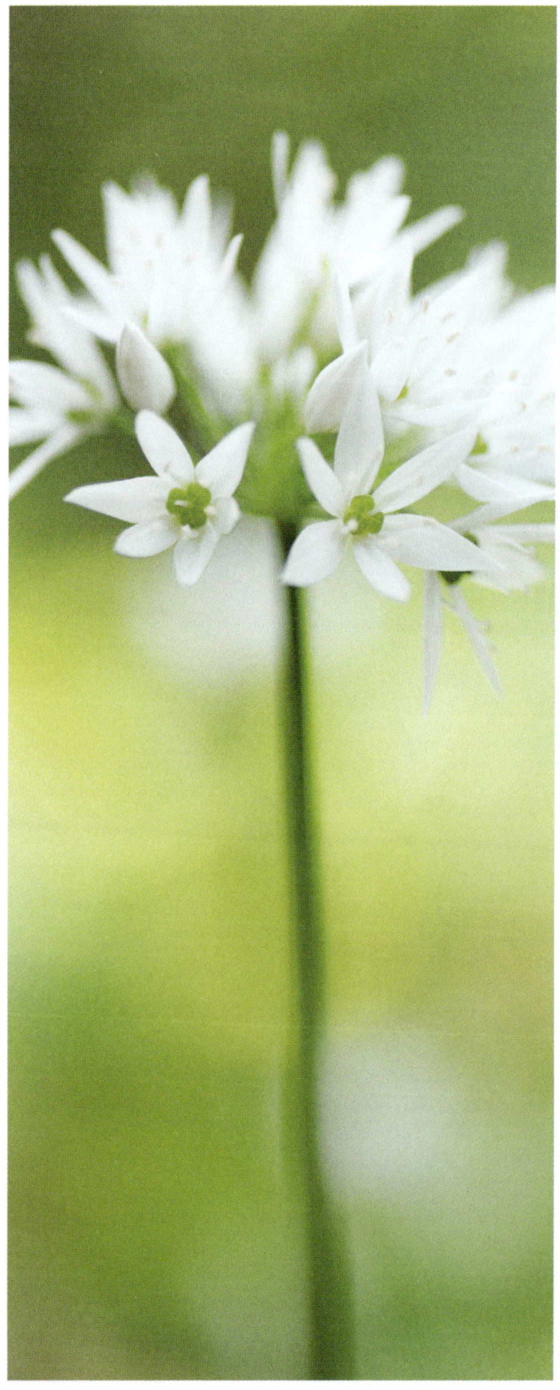

◄ Cropping is a more sensible option for delicate subjects that may move as you shoot a sequence.

THE PROCESS

1 Fit your camera to the tripod vertically if shooting a horizontal panoramic, or horizontally if shooting vertically.

2 Set the camera to Manual exposure mode and a fixed ISO, then select a White Balance preset suitable for the ambient lighting.

3 Position the camera to the left edge of where you want the panoramic to start.

4 Set the shutter speed and aperture and manually focus the lens.

5 Shoot the image using either a remote release or by selecting the self-timer facility.

6 Pan the camera right or move it right on a focusing rail if fitted. Ideally you want there to be overlap of roughly one-third with the previous shot.

7 Repeat steps 3 and 4 until you reach the far-right edge of the planned panoramic.

8 Import your images into postproduction software that supports panoramic stitching and creates the panoramic.

9 Crop the image to suit.

The simplest way to create a panoramic is to crop an image. However, this will reduce the resolution of the image and so it isn't ideal. Another method is to create a stitched panoramic, created by blending a series of images shot while moving the camera from left to right or up and down. The downside to this method is that is takes time to shoot and, ideally, nothing in the scene should move as you shoot. Some cameras will automatically generate a panoramic image after completion. For those without that facility you would need to import the images into suitable postproduction software to create the stitched panoramic. The result in either case is a high-resolution image that can be printed at a far larger scale without loss of quality compared to a cropped panoramic.

To complete this assignment, shoot a series of panoramic images, either cropped or created by stitching. Think carefully about composition and the type of subject you think is suitable.

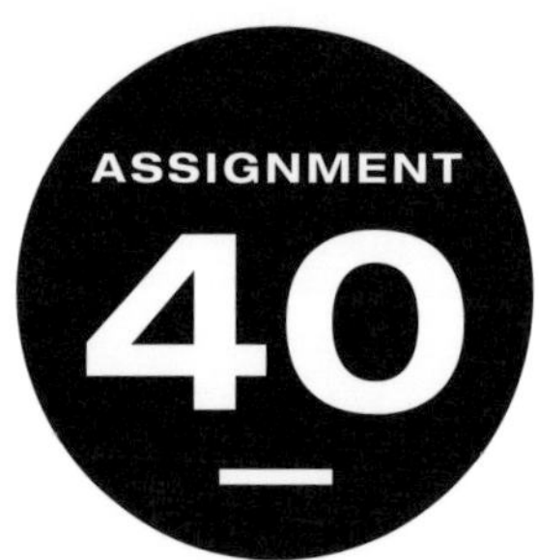

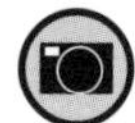
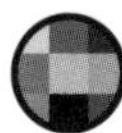

SPECIAL KIT

- Tripod

- Lamp and flash or other lighting

TIPS

- White Balance can also be altered in postproduction if you shoot in Raw.

- A colored reflector can be used to add a particular color into the shadows.

▶ *A more extreme effect can be achieved by using two gelled flashes or studio lights. Primary colors work well together, such as red and blue as used here.*

WARM AND COOL

A simple technique to introduce visual contrast (see assignment 34) into an image is to light a scene using multiple light sources, each with a different color temperature. Light sources can be broadly thought of as warm, neutral, or cool, depending on their color temperature. Household bulbs usually emit warm light, with a color temperature in the 2700–4500°K range. Summer sunlight in a cloudless sky at midday and flash are both neutral in color, with a color temperature of 5500–5700°K. Overcast and shade light is cool, between 6000–7500°K, depending on conditions.

We generally expect highlights to be warm and shadows to be cool. One way to achieve this is using light from a lamp as the main source of illumination and filling in the shadows with flash. (White Balance should be set to Incandescent.) However, photography is about being creative and there's no reason for sticking with warm highlights and cool shadows. For this assignment, experiment with using mixed lighting to illuminate your macro subjects. Adjust White Balance too, using different presets as you shoot to see what effect this has on the images.

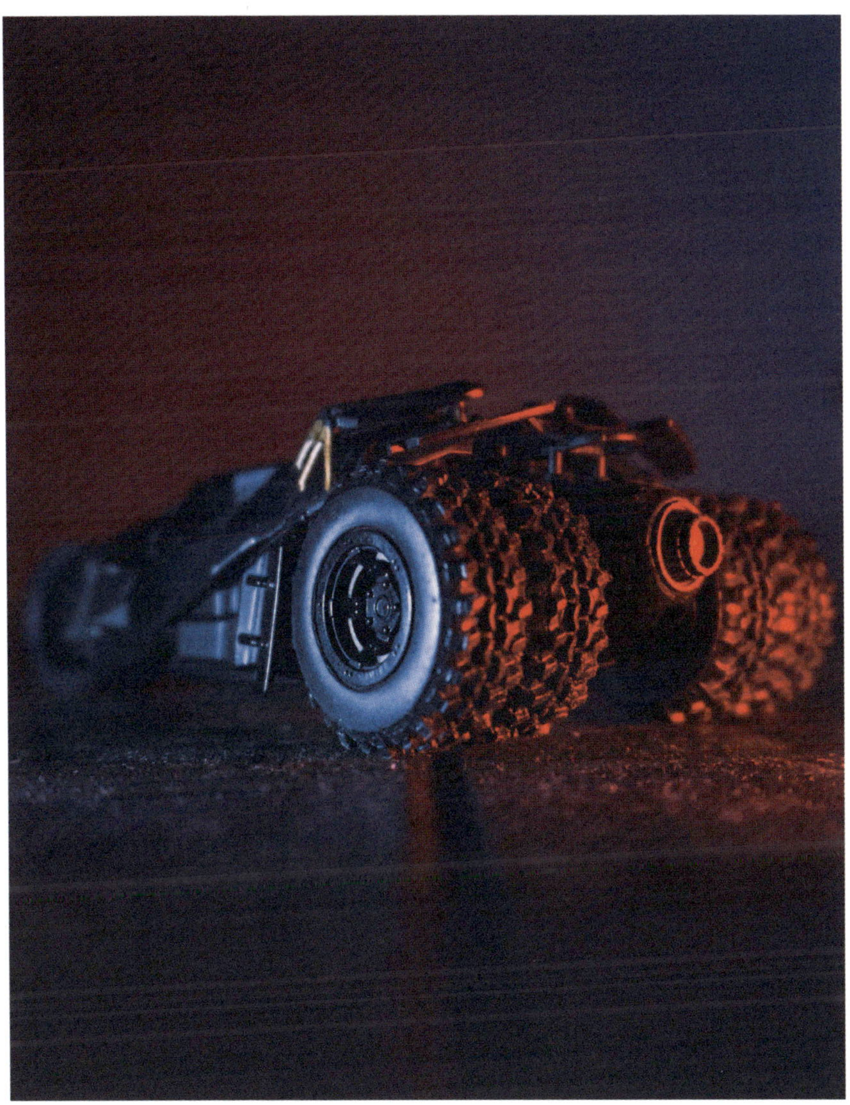

MACRO NOTES

Split-toning is a postproduction technique that can be used to create an effect similar to using two light sources. It's commonly used in black and white photography to add a subtle warmth to the highlights of an image and to add a coolness to the shadows. It can also be used in color photography, although the effect can look garish and unnatural if overdone.

▶ *Having the subject look away from the camera will add an air of mystery to the shot.*

THE EYES HAVE IT

Human and animal eyes are surprisingly detailed and colorful, which makes them a wonderful subject for macro photography. One important factor when photographing eyes is accurate focusing. We tend to look at the center of the eye first: at the iris, a ring of colorful muscle cells, and at the light-gathering pupil. Both of these should be sharp, otherwise the photo will look odd and slightly disturbing.

Lighting is important too. Eyes in a photo can look strangely lifeless if there's no catchlight, which is a bright highlight from a nearby light source. Lighting, whether ambient or from flash or a studio light, should be bright enough to allow the use of a fast shutter speed and low ISO rating, but not so bright as to dazzle the subject. (A fast shutter speed is particularly important when shooting the eyes of animals, who are less likely to stay still as you shoot.)

Eyes are said to be the windows to the soul, as they convey so much of what a person is thinking or feeling. Your assignment is to create a small portfolio of eye photos. They can be those of family, friends, models, or even your own. If your subjects are willing, try shooting the eyes in a number of different ways, such as unadorned and with makeup, facing the camera directly and looking away.

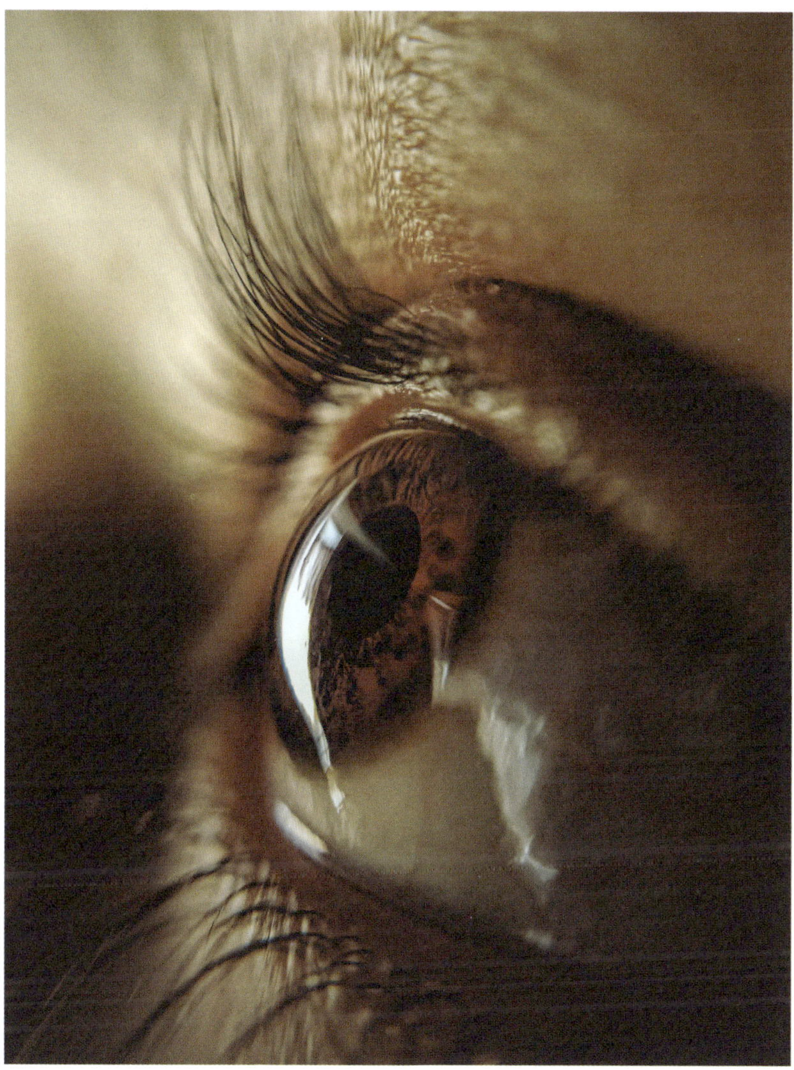

MACRO NOTES

Red eye is caused by light from a flash bouncing off the back of an eye, picking up the color of blood vessels in the fundus as it does so. Some flashes have a "red-eye removal" mode that works by pulsing light from the flash before the main exposure, which causes the pupil in the subject's eye to narrow.

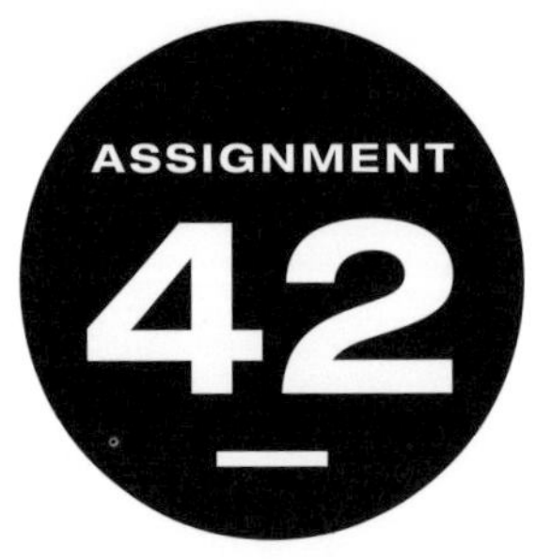

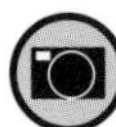
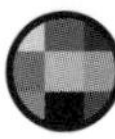

TIPS

- A tablet can also be used as a backlighting source when the screen is filled with a pure white image.

- Use a wide aperture to minimize depth-of-field when using a window as a backlighting source. This will ensure that any potentially distracting background will be out of focus.

TRANSLUCENCY

The word translucent comes from the Latin words trans for through and lucere for to shine. Translucent objects are at their most photogenic when illuminated by backlighting. This makes their color more vibrant and intense. A lightbox is the ideal tool to shoot macro images of translucent objects. Lightboxes are bright, and provide stable and consistent lighting. Flash, studio lighting, and windows can also be used to provide backlighting.

To complete this assignment, find and shoot a series of translucent objects. These can be natural subjects, such as leaves, or artificial, such as beads. The key is to find objects that are colorful and that are likely to glow vibrantly when backlit. Backlighting can also help to reveal structure within a translucent object, so consider this too when shooting the assignment. The images could be straight record shots of your chosen subject, but could also be abstract and purely about color. The idea is to have fun as you shoot.

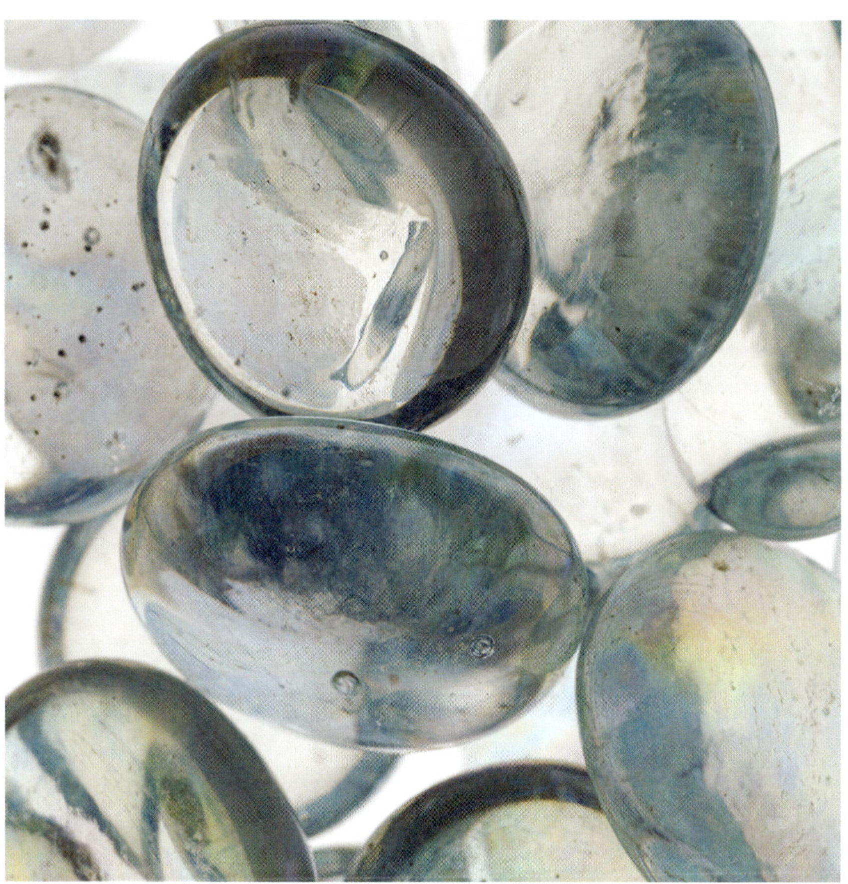

ASSIGNMENT JOURNAL

▲ *Expose for your objects and don't worry
if any gaps around the object burn out.
A pure white background will help color
stand out more.*

MACRO NOTES

The traditional photography lightbox was
originally designed to view and assess
film negatives and slides. Lightboxes
are typically daylight-balanced, so the
Daylight White Balance preset should
be selected when a lightbox is used as
the light source.

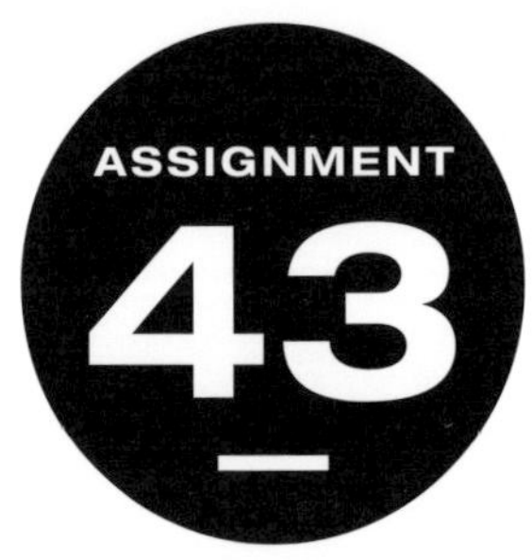

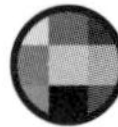

SPECIAL KIT

- Tripod
- Studio light or off-camera flash

TIPS

- Perfect White Balance is key for accurate color. Don't mix light sources with different Kelvin settings unless for effect.
- Using a wide aperture is a simple way to place emphasis on the product by minimizing depth-of-field.

PRODUCT PHOTOGRAPHY

Photographs of commercial products are everywhere: in magazines, on billboards, and on retail websites. Good product photography should make you pause and at least wonder briefly whether this is a product that would be suitable for you. Brands with big advertising budgets will employ not just a photographer but art directors and stylists too. These people all work in concert to create the perfect image of the product.

Products are often combined with a few relevant props that help to tell the story of that product. However, the product is always the focal point of the shot. A relevant background will also help to set the scene but should never overpower the product. Products are usually shot straight on with the camera at the same level. They are rarely shot with a wide-angle lens, shooting with a short telephoto is more common. The perspective from the use of a telephoto lens (and the distance this places between the camera and the subject) is visually pleasing and naturalistic.

For this assignment, read through a variety of lifestyle magazines, looking closely at the product shots. Pick out three that you particularly like and carefully analyze them to work out how they were lit and composed. Try to replicate the shots for yourself using similar subjects. Use a tripod so that you can experiment with the lighting and composition as you shoot.

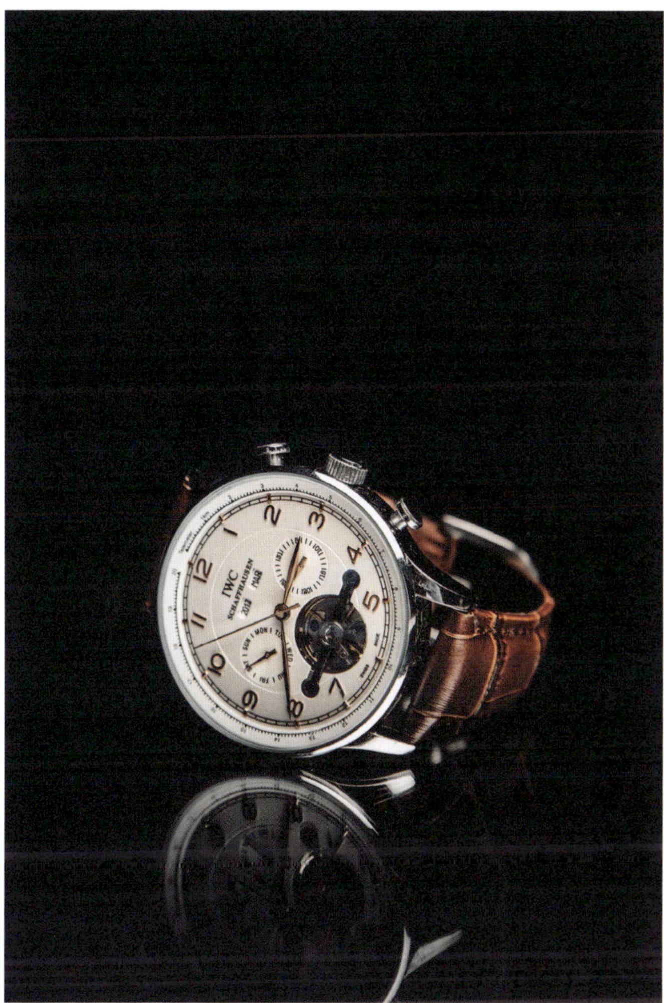

▲ *Photos of products are often overlaid with text. For this reason, products are often shot surrounded with empty space where the text will ultimately be placed.*

MACRO NOTES

A color checker is a printed grid of color patches shot in the same light and with the same exposure as the product. The image featuring the color checker is then used to set the White Balance and check color accuracy of the product images in postproduction.

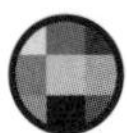

SPECIAL KIT

- Tripod
- Black background
- Off-camera flash or a studio light fitted with a softbox
- Soap and water solution
- Small bowl
- Straw
- Remote release

TIPS

- Black velvet is very light-absorbent and ideal when a black background is required.
- Use the Vivid Picture Style to enhance the color of the soap bubble.
- Select spot metering and set exposure by metering from the soap bubble.

SOAP BUBBLES

Soap bubbles are surprisingly complex things, made up of three separate layers: a thin film of water sandwiched between an outer and inner layer of soap molecules. The colors on the surface of a bubble are created by the interference of wavelengths of light as the light reflects off the two soap layers.

How thick or otherwise the layers of soap are determines the range of visible colors. When a bubble is first blown the soap layers are relatively thick and the bubble is at its most colorful. As the water in the bubble evaporates, fewer and fewer colors can be seen until, when there is not enough water in the bubble to maintain surface tension, the bubble final bursts.

Creating images of soap bubbles requires preparation beforehand and a certain amount of patience during the shooting—soap bubbles don't last long, particularly when in a hot room. For this assignment create a short sequence of soap bubble images. Try shooting at different distances from the soap bubbles, as well as varying the ratio of soap to water in the soap solution.

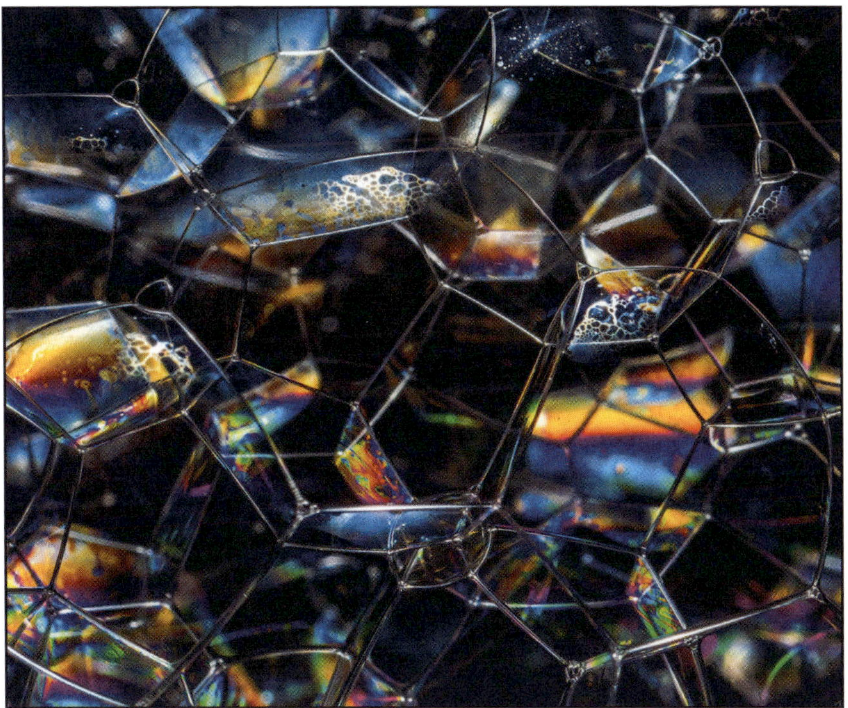

▲ *A mass of soap bubbles will create interesting polygonal shapes as well as vibrant colors.*

MACRO NOTES

A camera's spot meter measures exposure from a very small percentage of the image area. This is usually either at the center of the frame or from a specific area such as the focus point. Spot metering is ideal when there are large areas of black in a shot that could otherwise cause overexposure.

THE PROCESS

1 Place a small bowl filled with soap and water solution in front of a black background with the softbox roughly 4–8in (10–20cm) above the bowl and facing downward.

2 Select a small aperture, such as f/11 or f/16.

3 Focus manually on the front of the bowl.

4 Use the straw to gently blow a bubble in the soap and water solution.

5 Adjust focus if necessary, wait a few seconds, and then take a shot.

6 The colors will continually change, so take more shots until the bubble finally bursts.

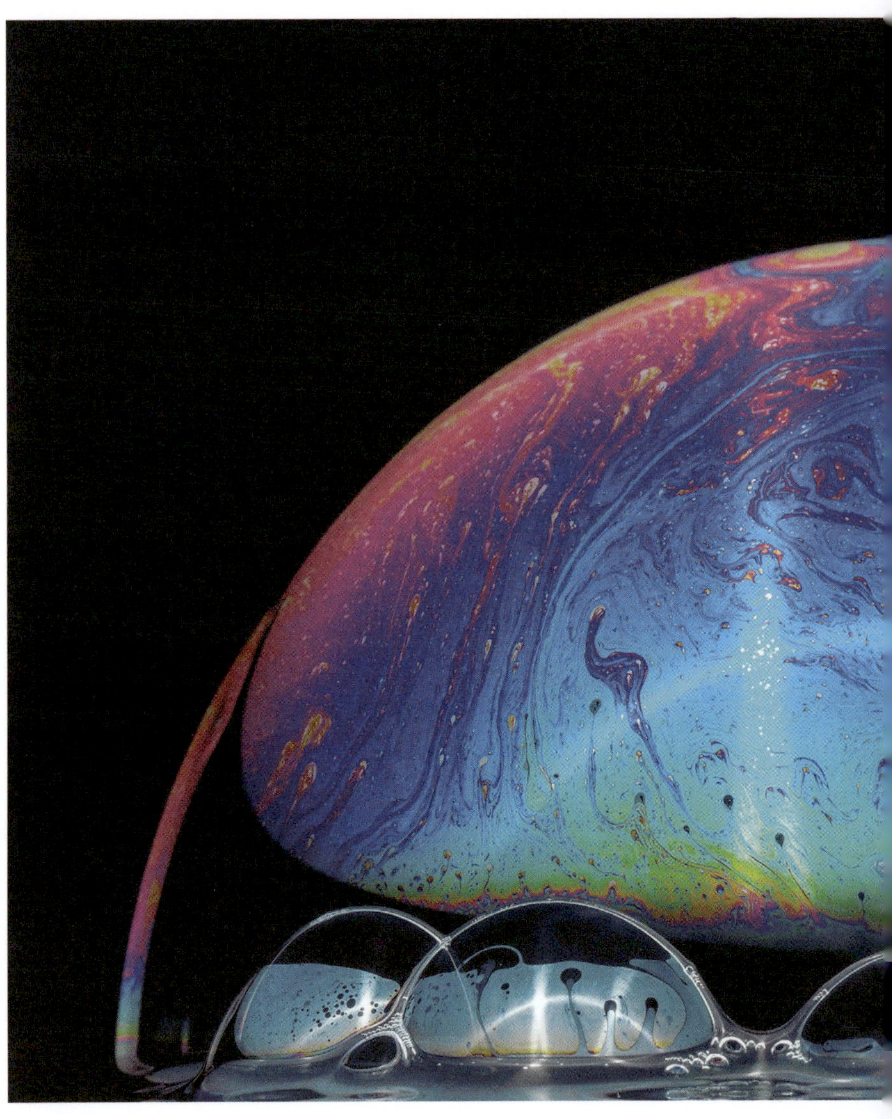

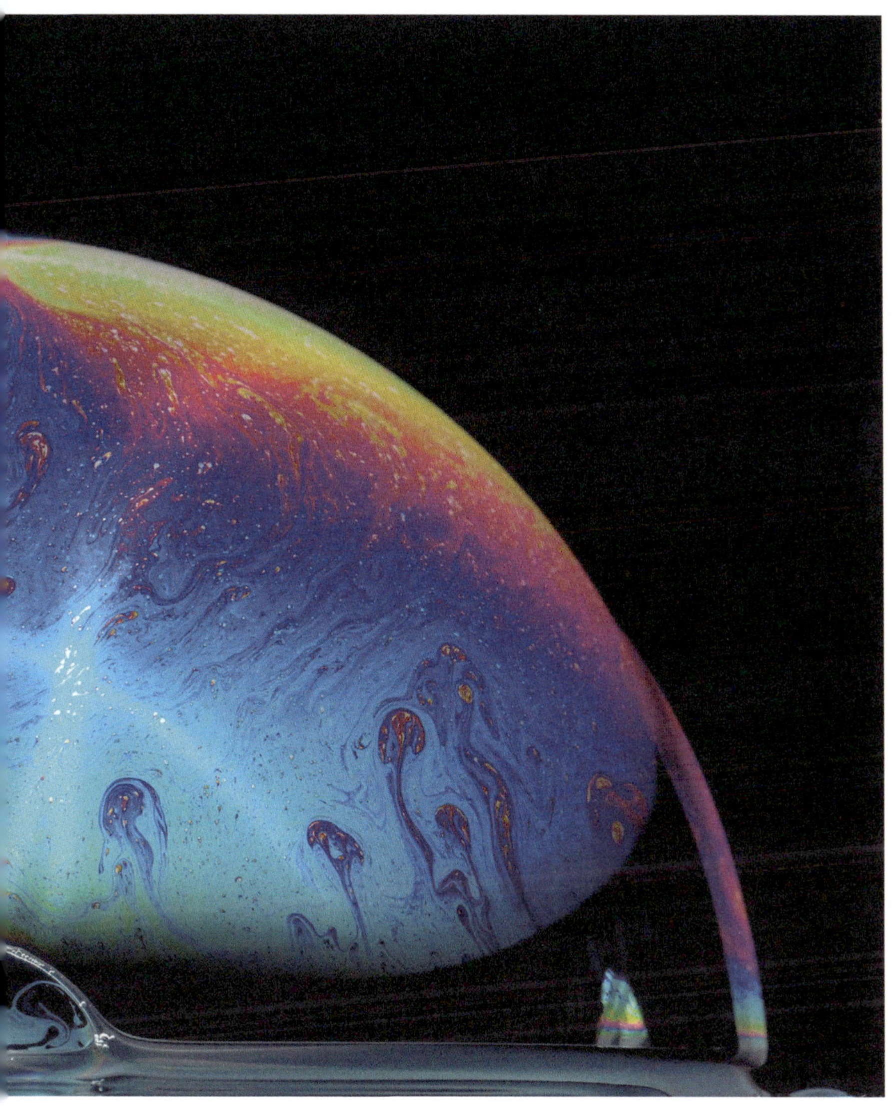

▲ *Black velvet is very light-absorbent and ideal when a deep black background is required.*

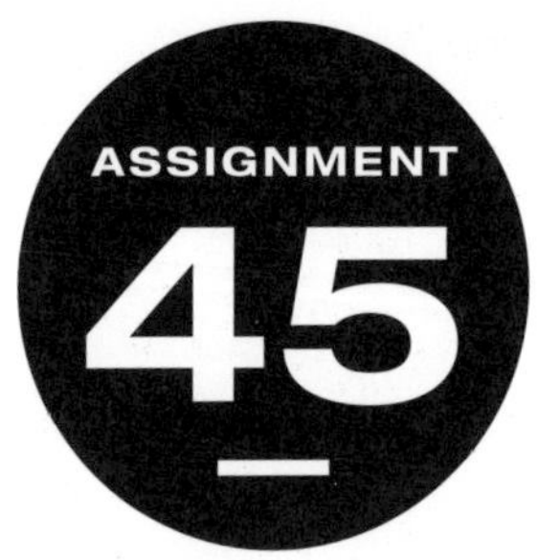

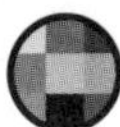
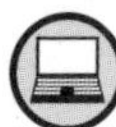

TIPS

- Hard light (see assignment 16) works well for black and white photography.

- Subjects that are already largely monochromatic are ideal for the black and white treatment.

▶ *Effects such as grain and vignetting arguably work better when applied to black and white images rather than color.*

BLACK AND WHITE

Black and white photography has a timeless quality that is still relevant and appealing, even in the twenty-first century. To create a successful black and white image, you need to be aware of factors such as highlights and shadows, as well as the shape of your subject and its surface texture. For this reason, some subjects don't suit the monochrome treatment. Anything that relies purely on color for impact is likely to be unsuitable.

Digital cameras make it easier to judge whether a subject works in black and white or not. All cameras have a black and white Picture Style (often referred to as Monochrome). Selecting this option will display a monochrome image in LiveView on the rear screen, or in the EVF of a mirrorless camera.

Shooting Raw is a better option than JPEG when creating black and white images. With Raw, even when the Monochrome profile is selected, the color information is retained. JPEG files have all the color stripped out so there is no going back later. Ultimately, converting a color image to black and white in postproduction will give you greater control over the process.

For this assignment, choose subjects that will work well when shot in black and white, thinking carefully about how they are lit. Create a small portfolio of the ten most successful images.

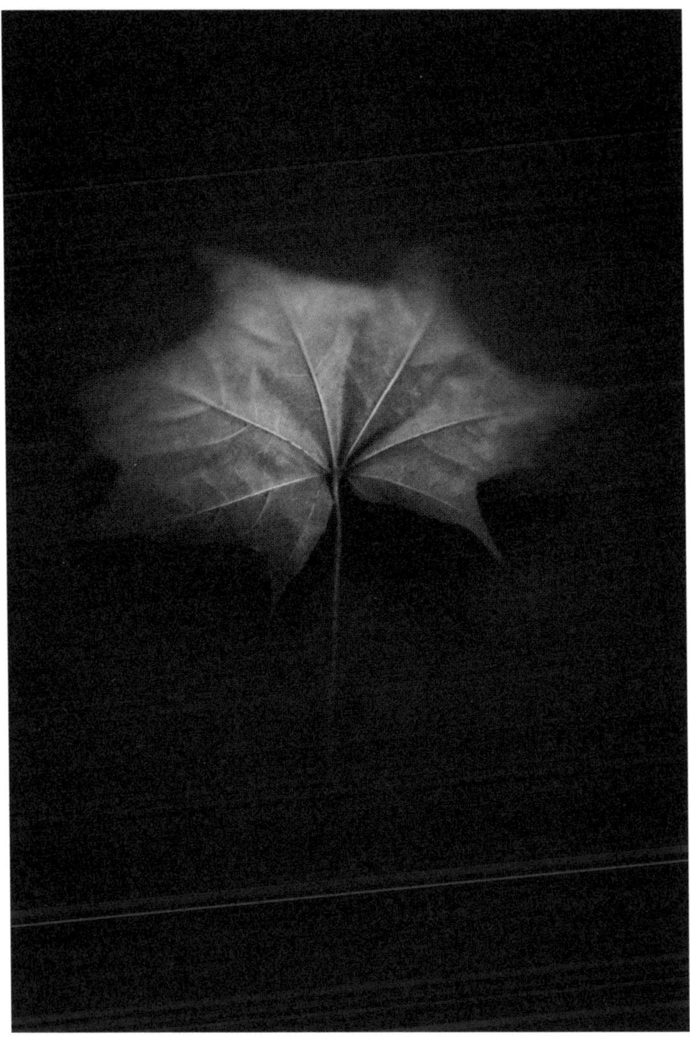

MACRO NOTES

The Monochrome Picture Style often has a Filter option where you can
select between Yellow, Orange, Red, and Green. These options lighten
similar colors in the image and darken those on the opposite side of
a standard color wheel: blues are darkened when the Yellow, Orange,
and Red filters are selected, and blue-purple when Green is used. The
options can help separate tones that would otherwise look very similar
in brightness when converted to black and white.

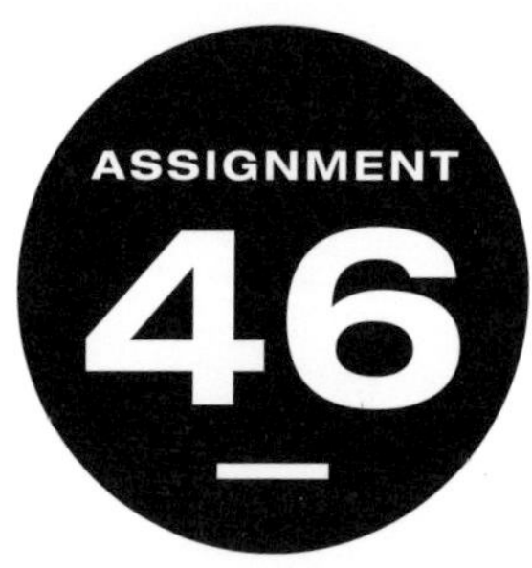

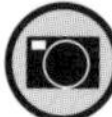

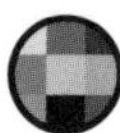

SPECIAL KIT

- Tripod

TIPS

- Thoroughly clean your chosen subject beforehand to remove any blemishes or stains.

- Use food as props and to add color to shots.

ASSIGNMENT JOURNAL

MACRO NOTES

A specular highlight is an intense but generally small bright reflection from a point light source seen on the surface of shiny objects. The intensity of specular highlights can be reduced by softening the light source through the use of a diffuser or reflector.

▶ *Brightly-colored plastic utensils are fun but need to be shot when brand new, as they quickly scratch and discolor.*

KITCHEN UTENSILS

A kitchen is a great place to find subjects suitable for macro photography. A rummage through drawers in a kitchen is likely to produce a wide variety of implements that are visually distinctive and interesting. Kitchens often provide interesting backdrops too, including countertops and tiles, as well as chopping boards, crockery, and table mats.

Many kitchen implements are metal and so will be highly reflective. Using soft light, from a softbox or a north-facing window, will help reduce the appearance of distracting specular highlights. Using a telephoto or long focal length macro lens will also help to reduce the risk of you or your camera appearing in the reflections too. However, reflections can be used for effect. A patterned or colorful surface held out-of-frame over the subject will add visual interest to the shot. Carefully-controlled direct lighting can be used to create shadows that help define the form of the objects you use.

For this assignment, choose one kitchen implement. Shoot ten shots, varying the approach you take for each image. Shoot under different types of light and with different backgrounds. Try making relatively straight shots of your chosen subject, as well as shooting in a more abstract way, exploring the form and texture of the implement.

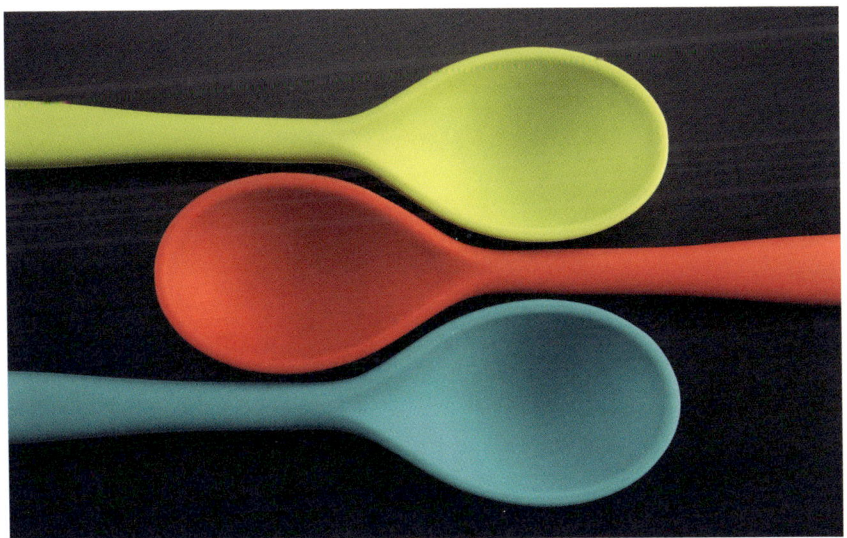

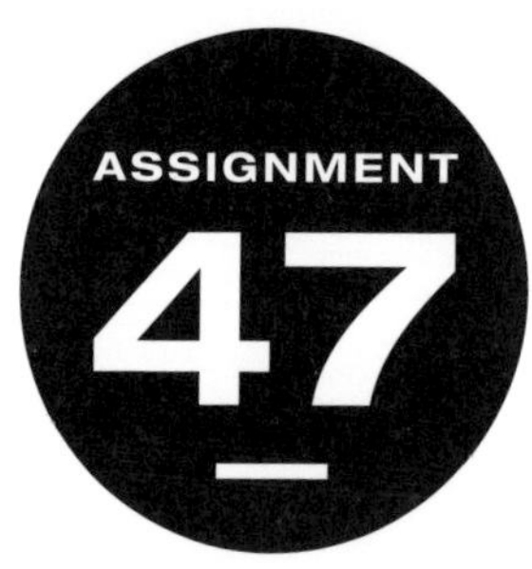

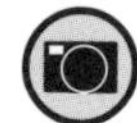
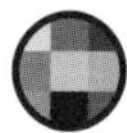

SPECIAL KIT

- Tripod
- Off-camera flash
- Bowl or dish
- Water
- Pipette filled with water

TIPS

- Add a drop of milk to the water in the bowl to make it a more uniform background.

- A shallow bowl of water will create a "crown" effect. Deeper water is more likely to produce a column.

▶ *Flash recycling time is shorter when low-power flash is used. This means you should be able to fire off several frames in rapid succession.*

WATER DROPLETS

The shapes made by droplets falling onto a pool of water are wonderfully photogenic. Capturing these shapes requires preparation but the technique is relatively simple. The shapes made by the droplets last a fraction of a second, so the first challenge is setting a short enough exposure to avoid motion blur. This is more easily achieved through the use of flash rather than a fast shutter speed.

Flash exposure is controlled by a variation in the length of time the flash is illuminated. As the power of a flash is lowered, the flash emits a shorter burst of light. To freeze movement effectively you would therefore use the lowest power setting that still results in the correct exposure. Manual flash exposure is better than TTL for this type of photography, as it gives you more control over the power of the flash.

For this assignment, shoot a series of water droplet images (explained overleaf). Experiment with composition and flash exposure. Try adding food dyes to the water to create different effects, as well as using other liquids.

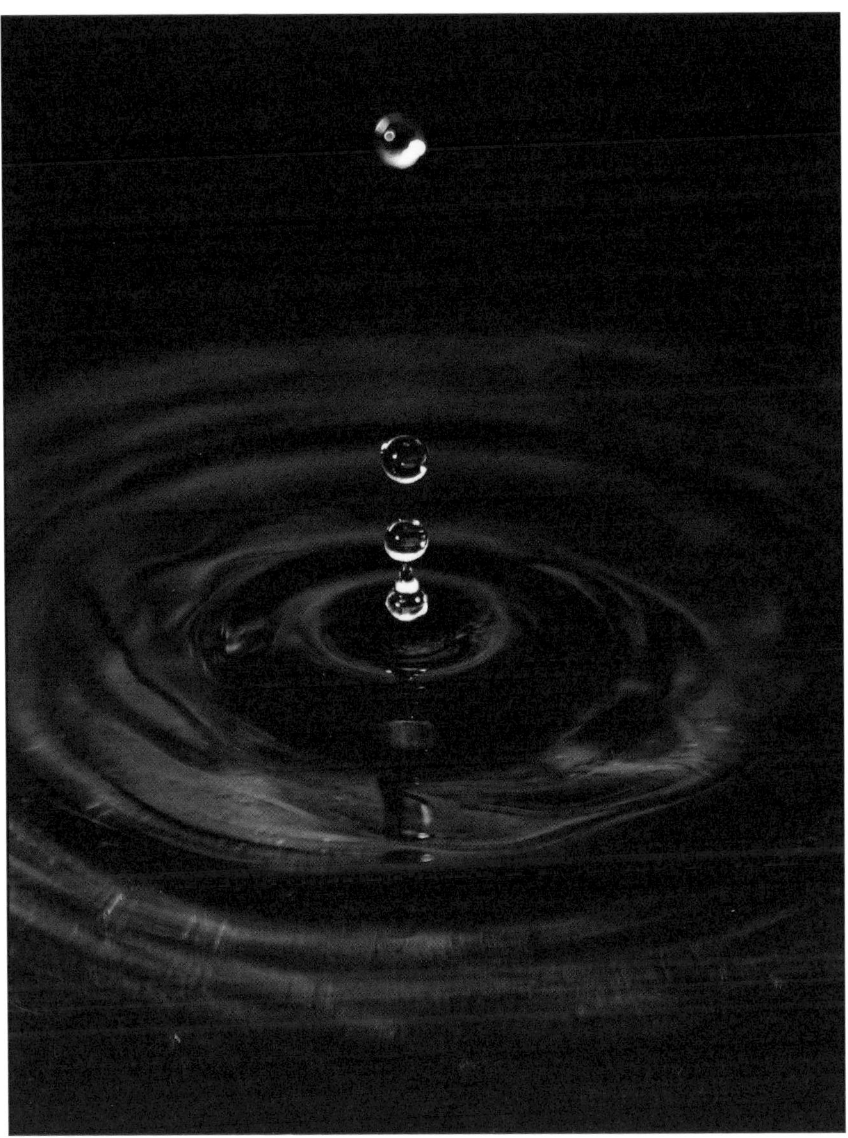

MACRO NOTES

Using flash at a lower power setting helps the flash to recharge more quickly too. This means that multiple flashes can be fired in rapid succession. The rate the flash recharges will also be improved by using a fresh set of batteries.

THE PROCESS

1 Add water to your bowl and position your camera—mounted on a tripod—close to the bowl.

2 Position your off-camera flash to the side of the bowl at 90° to the camera.

3 Focus manually on the surface of the water (use a finger held in position if you find focusing difficult). Note where you've focused.

4 Set the camera to Manual exposure mode. Select a low ISO rating and set the shutter speed to the sync speed of your camera.

5 Set a mid-range or small aperture. The aperture needs to be small enough that the scene would be underexposed without light from the flash.

6 With the flash set to Manual, select a power setting of 1/64 or 1/128.

7 Set the drive mode to Continuous.

8 Use the pipette to drip water where you focused the camera, firing the shutter as you do so.

9 Adjust the flash exposure if necessary and reshoot.

▲ *Use colored paper held over the bowl and out of shot to add color to the surface of the water.*

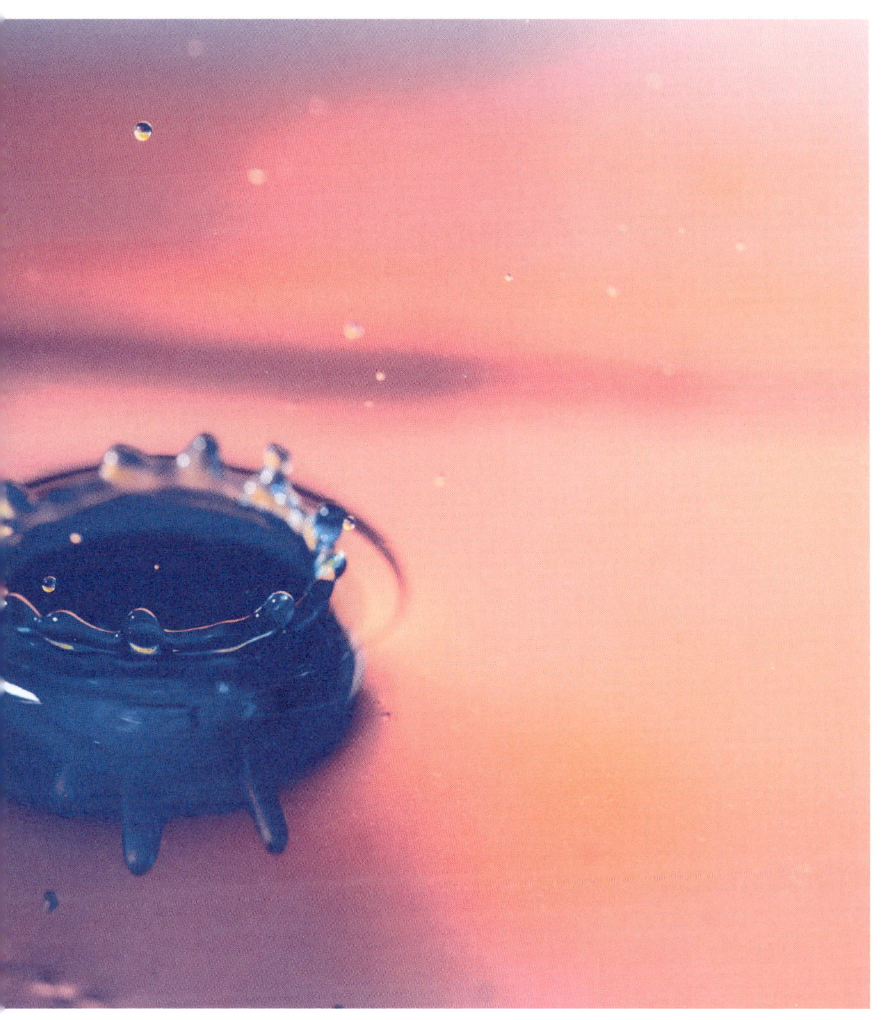

ASSIGNMENT JOURNAL

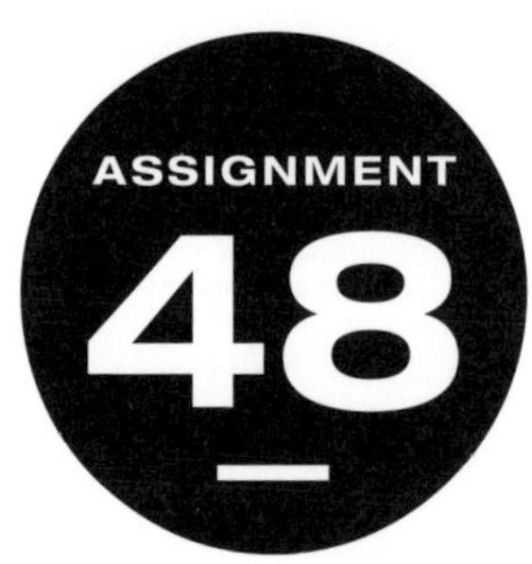

 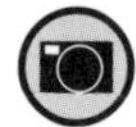
 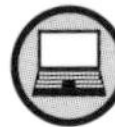

SPECIAL KIT

- Tripod
- Focusing rail
- Off-camera flash or studio lighting.
- Anaglyph glasses
- Computer

TIPS

- This technique can be combined with focus stacking (see assignment 49) to create images with greater sharpness through the image.
- Don't shoot objects straight on. Shoot them at an angle to create more depth.
- The distance you move the camera should be roughly the distance between the pupil's eyes.

INTO THE THIRD DIMENSION

Stereoscopic photography is the art of creating the illusion of depth through the viewing of two photos shot from slightly different positions. An anaglyph is a stereoscopic image created by combining two photos, one shot with a blue or cyan filter and the other with a red filter. When cyan/red 3D glasses are worn, the brain interprets these two images as a single three-dimensional image.

Creating three-dimensional macro images is straightforward but does require preparation and some patience. It also requires postproduction to combine the images you shoot into the final photo. The results are charming and have a slightly retro quality.

To complete this assignment, experiment with 3D macro photography (explained overleaf). Consider carefully what subjects will work best. Ideally, they should be objects that won't move as you shoot.

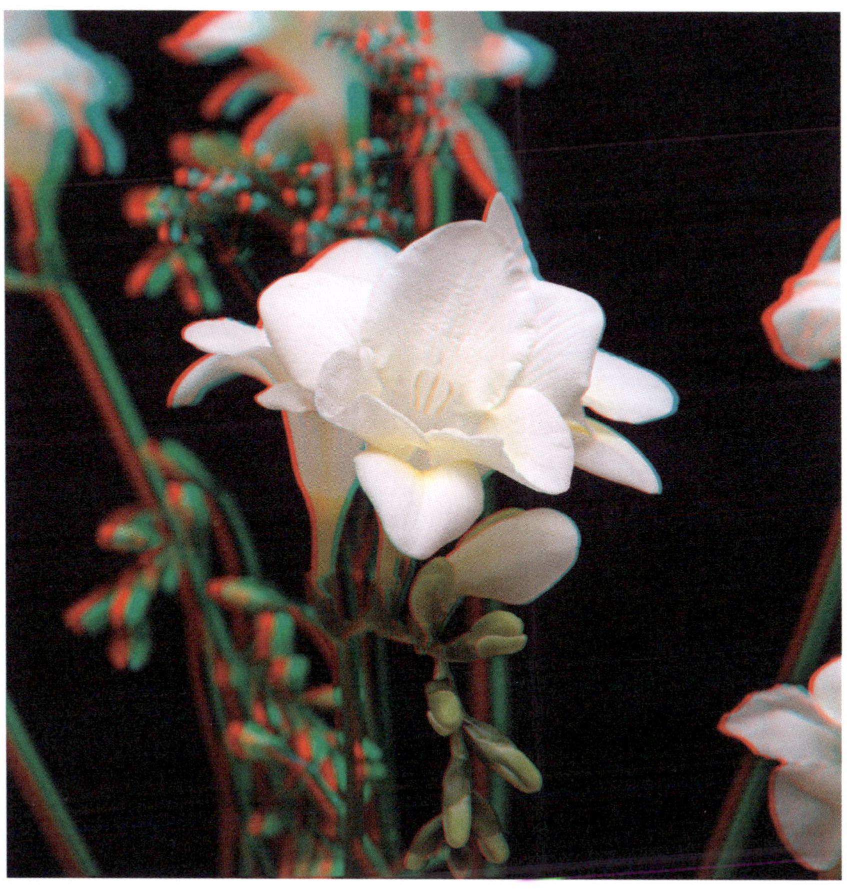

▲ *The stamens in this central flower are the focal point, so they were the point at which the two layers aligned exactly.*

MACRO NOTES

Stereoscopic viewers were incredibly popular during the Victorian period and intermittently popular ever since. The principle of shooting two images from slightly different positions is the same, but the results are more natural and don't rely on a red/blue color shift.

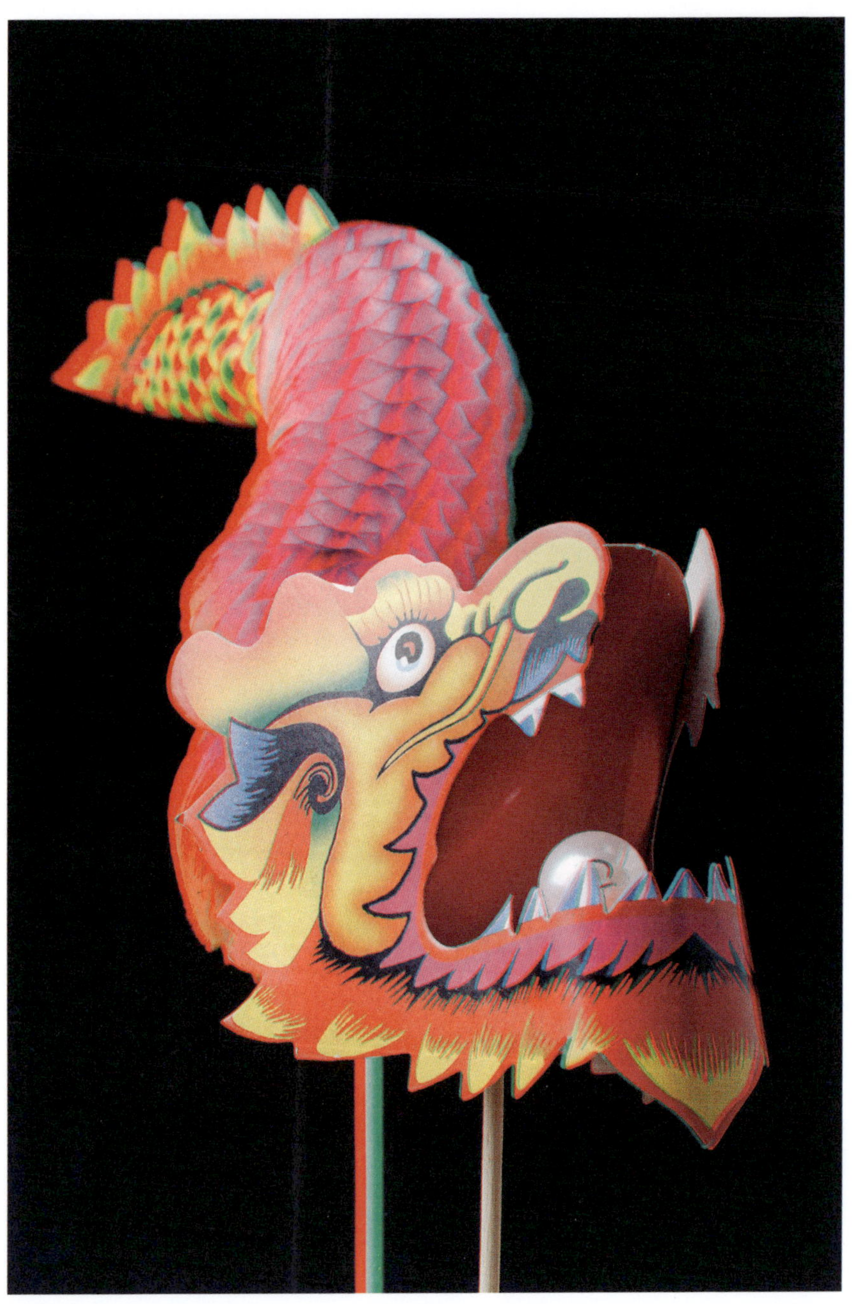

▲ *Leave plenty of space around your subject when shooting vertically to allow for the left to right movement of the camera, and then crop to suit afterward.*

THE PROCESS

1 Position your subject and set up the lighting.

2 Fit your camera to a focusing rail so that the camera is at 90° to the rail. (The camera will need to pan from side to side, rather than in and out.)

3 Fit the camera and focusing rail combination to a tripod and compose with your subject biased slightly to the left side of the frame. This will be the left eye image.

4 Set the camera to Aperture-priority mode and select a small aperture to maximize depth-of-field. Take the shot.

5 Carefully pan the camera to the right by two or three centimeters. Take a second shot. This will be the right eye image.

6 Import both images into your postproduction software and convert the first image you shot into a layer, naming it Left Eye.

7 Drag the second image you shot into the first as a layer and name it Right Eye. This layer should be uppermost in the layer stack.

8 Change the layer blending for the Left Eye layer so that only the Red channel is displayed and the layer blending for the Right Eye layer so that only the Blue and Green channels are displayed.

9 Look at the image through your 3D glasses to see how well the effect works. If necessary, move one of the layers left or right until one point in that layer aligns with the same point in the other layer.

ASSIGNMENT JOURNAL

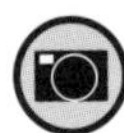

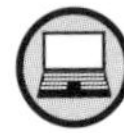

SPECIAL KIT

- Tripod

- Focus stacking software

- Remote release

TIPS

- Shoot using Manual exposure mode or lock exposure so that the exposure stays constant as you shoot.

- Use a remote release so that you touch the camera as little as possible and avoid knocking it.

STACKED

One of the real challenges when shooting macro is a lack of depth-of-field. Even when a lens is stopped down to its smallest aperture, depth-of-field may not be sufficient to render a subject sharp from front to back. Stopping down the aperture may also extend shutter speeds to potentially unacceptable lengths. Lenses are also not at their best optically when stopped down to their smallest aperture.

A solution is focus stacking. This is a technique where a series of images are captured with the focus point altered between each shot. The sequence is then combined in focus stacking software to create a final image that's sharp from back to front. As shooting a sequence takes time, it's a technique that's ideally suited to subjects that don't move. However, with practice it can be used on living subjects, such as insects. Some cameras offer options to automate the adjustment of focus, making focus stacking easier to shoot and more rapid.

Your brief for this assignment is to try focus stacking using a suitable still-life subject (explained overleaf). Think about how many shots will be needed to create a sequence, and how far each focus step needs to be.

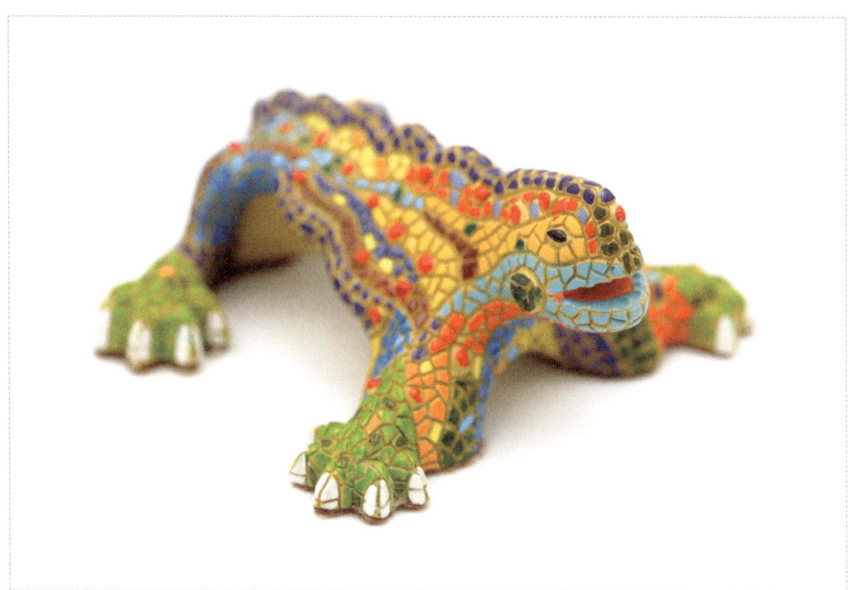

▲ *Care was taken to ensure that the closest part of the subject was pin sharp in the first shot. This was achieved through the use of focus peaking as a visual guide as the focus ring was slowly turned.*

▼ *Focus peaking combined with depth-of-field preview will also help to determine how many shots will be needed to create the final image. The greater the depth-of-field in each shot, the fewer photos you'll need to shoot.*

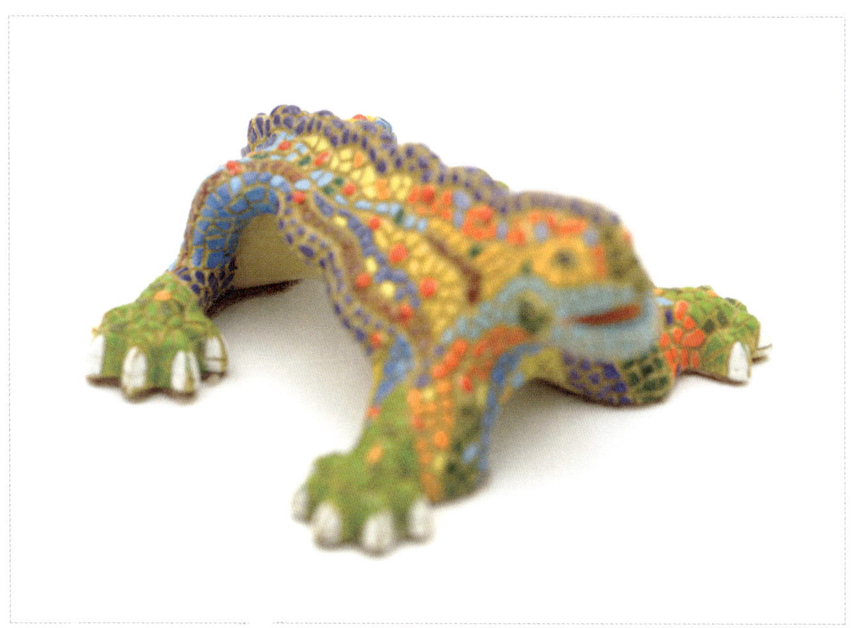

THE PROCESS

1 Compose the shot with the camera mounted on a tripod.

2 Select a mid-range aperture, such as f/8.

3 Using manual focus, focus on the front of the subject and shoot.

4 Focus slightly farther back along the subject and take another shot. Repeat until you reach the rear of the subject.

5 Import the sequence of images into your focus stacking software.

6 Create the stacked image.

MACRO NOTES

A quirk of some lenses is known as focus breathing. This is when the focal length of the lens changes as the focus distance is altered. This can happen even when shooting with a prime lens, including macro lenses. When shooting a focus stacked sequence, the subject will appear to change size through the sequence. For this reason, don't crop in too tightly when composing the shot and allow plenty of space around the subject.

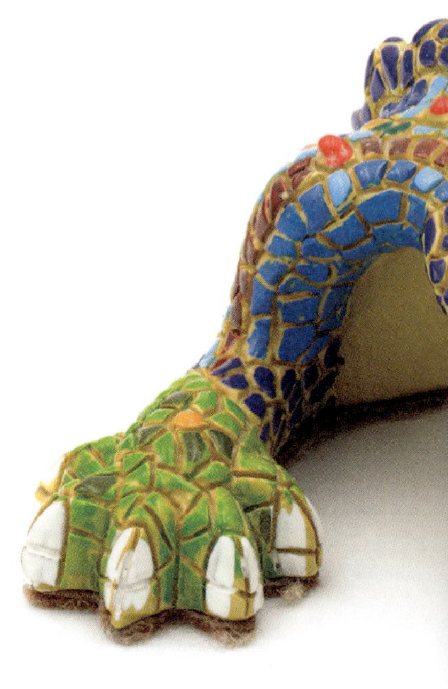

▶ *The resulting image, which combines the relevant areas from both images. The aim is to make the edits as subtle as you can.*

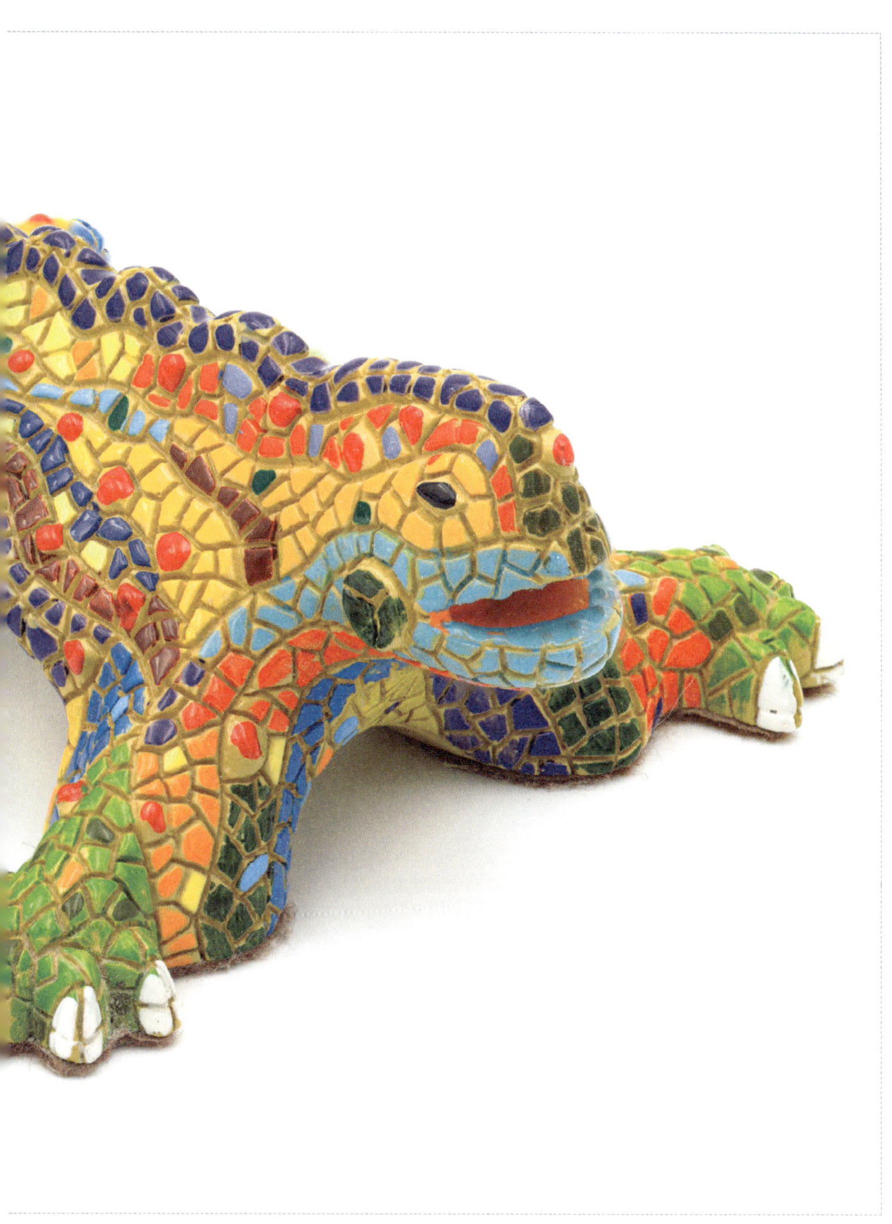

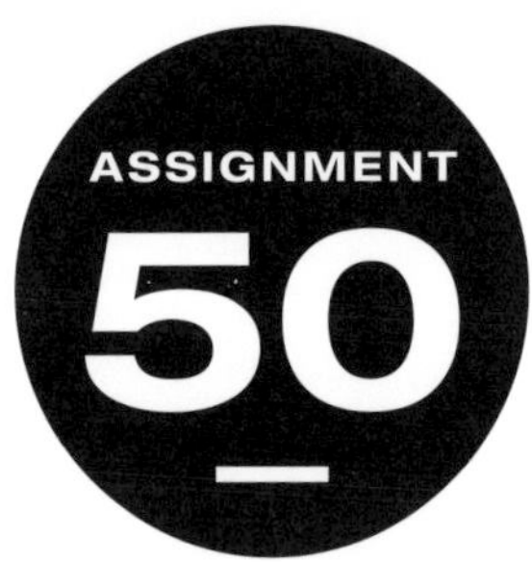

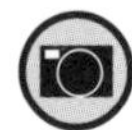
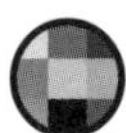

SPECIAL KIT

- Tripod

- Off-camera flash or studio light inside a soft box

- Large sheet of card

- Smaller sheets of card to use as reflectors

TIPS

- Clean the instrument before shooting to remove any distracting fingerprints or marks.

- Use a polarizing filter to reduce distracting reflections on wooden instruments.

MUSICAL INSTRUMENTS

Musical instruments come in all shapes and sizes and are made from a variety of different materials. For close-up and macro photography, brass and woodwind instruments are particularly rich in potential; the valve mechanisms and details such as the mouthpiece or reeds are very photogenic. The details of stringed instruments, such as the tuning pegs, are equally worth photographing, as are the materials used to make the instrument, such as the grain of the wood.

Brass instruments introduce the problems of reflections and lighting. Shooting through a lens-sized hole in a large sheet of card will help prevent you or your camera from being reflected in the metal surface of the instrument. Reflections do help to add interest to photographs of metal objects, however. Strips of white or black card placed close to the instrument can be used to create visual interest on what could otherwise be a plain surface. Shooting with a soft light source will help prevent intensely bright highlights.

Your brief for this assignment is to shoot a series of photos of a musical instrument, varying how you light and compose your shots as you do so. If you don't own a musical instrument, consider asking at a local church or concert venue to shoot an instrument there.

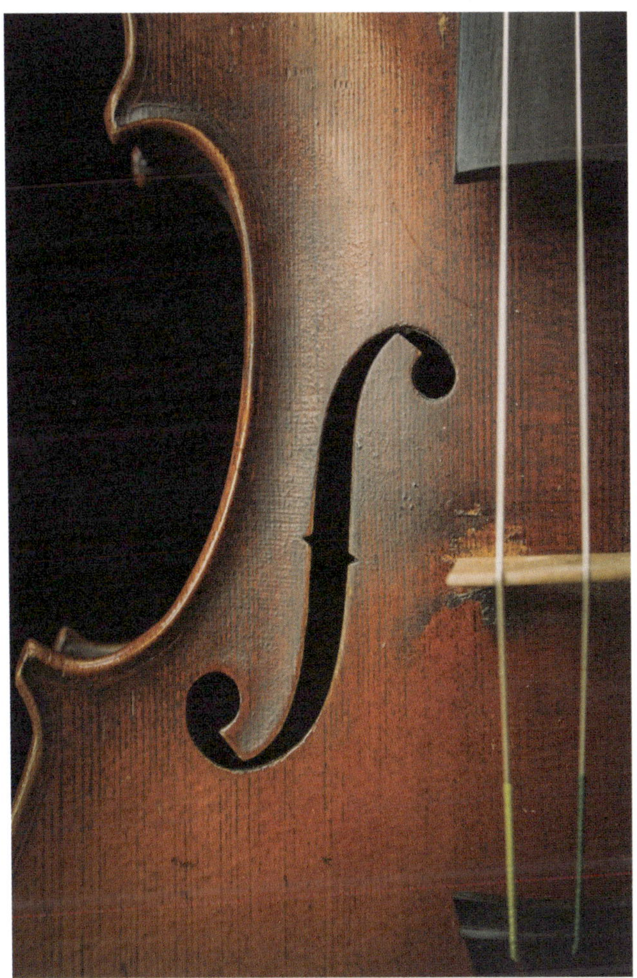

▲ *Think carefully about the background and either make it relevant to what you shoot or use a plain color.*

MACRO NOTES

Shooting handheld is far more spontaneous than using a tripod. For this kind of project, it's often easier to position the camera too. However, camera shake can be an issue even when image stabilization is active. Use a higher shutter speed than you would when shooting non-macro shots, increasing the ISO rating if necessary.

SPECIAL KIT

- Tripod
- Bellows
- Prime lens

TIPS

- Use a remote release or self-timer to avoid the risk of camera shake when the shutter fires.
- Depth-of-field will be shallow, so consider using the focus stacking technique (see assignment 49).

▼ *This stamp was placed under glass to keep it perfectly flat during the exposure. Any slight curvature would have resulted in part of the image being out-of-focus.*

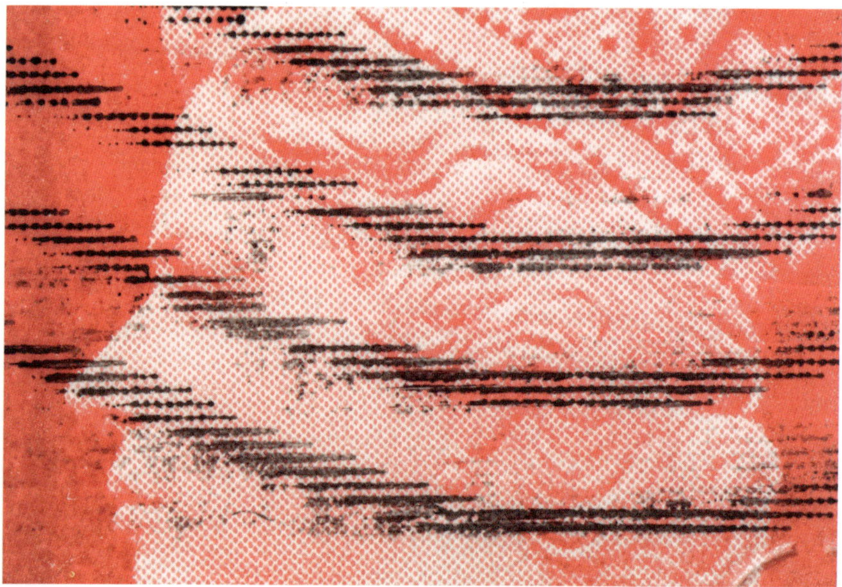

BELLOWS

Bellows look quaintly old-fashioned, but—when coupled with the right lens—they can be used to create images greater than 1x magnification, often significantly more. A set of bellows is essentially a more sophisticated type of extension ring, but one in which the amount of extension is variable and so more controllable.

Bellows are available for long-established lens mounts or readily adapted to fit more recent types. Some older bellows use the M42 mount that can also be adapted to fit virtually all current lens mounts. While versatile, there a few downsides to using bellows. They are cumbersome to use and are often heavy. Using a sturdy tripod is essential to avoid camera shake. There will also be no electronic connection between the lens at the front of the bellows and the camera. This can be overcome by using lenses that feature an aperture ring that allows you to control exposure and depth-of-field. Shorter focal length prime lenses work best with bellows, typically in the 28 to 50mm range.

For this assignment, use a set of bellows to create a short series of extreme magnification images. Work through any practical problems you may encounter, such as lighting and exposure.

MACRO NOTES

The M42 lens mount dates back to the late 1930s. Unlike today's bayonet lens mounts, M42 lenses are screwed into place. All M42 lenses are manual focus only and feature an aperture ring, which makes them ideal in combination with a set of bellows. Production of M42 lenses only ended in the 1980s, so there are plenty to be found second-hand for very little money.

ASSIGNMENT JOURNAL

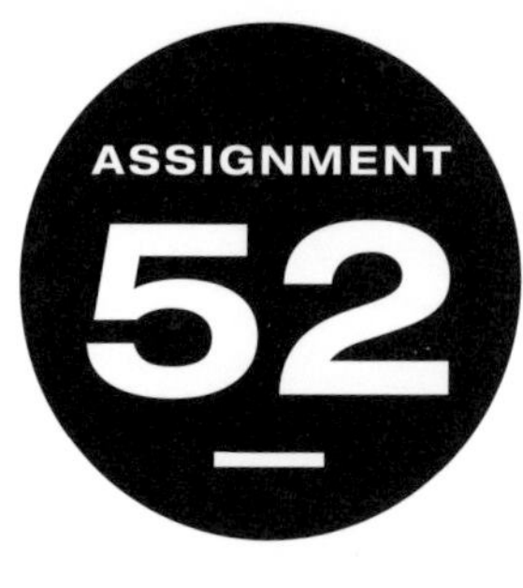

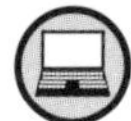

SPECIAL KIT

- PC or laptop

- Cellphone or tablet

TIPS

- Post personal stories about how you decided what to shoot and where you shot it too. People like stories that they can relate to.

- Post one photo a day at most. Too many posts will put off some people.

SOCIAL MEDIA

The quickest way to improve at something is to get honest and constructive feedback. Family and friends may be convenient, but they're more likely to be too kind when discussing your work. Posting on social media is a better way to solicit opinions and meet like-minded people. Instagram is currently one of the most popular ways to share online. The one drawback is that photos can only be posted via the Instagram app rather than through a website. Flickr is less popular than it once was but has the advantage that photos can be easily posted via a browser.

Building up a following can take time. Following other photographers, particularly those interested in the same subjects as you, is one way to get noticed. Adding relevant hashtags to your photos will allow other people to find your photos. A hashtag is a single word or phrase (with no spaces) preceded by a #, such as #macrophotography. Posting images that are less than perfect and inviting comments works well too. Trolling, when people post nasty or abusive comments, is fortunately rare. People, on the whole, are generally respectful and helpful.

For your final assignment open a social media account, if you don't have one already. Post photos and invite comments. Look at the work of other photographers and ask questions of them about their work.

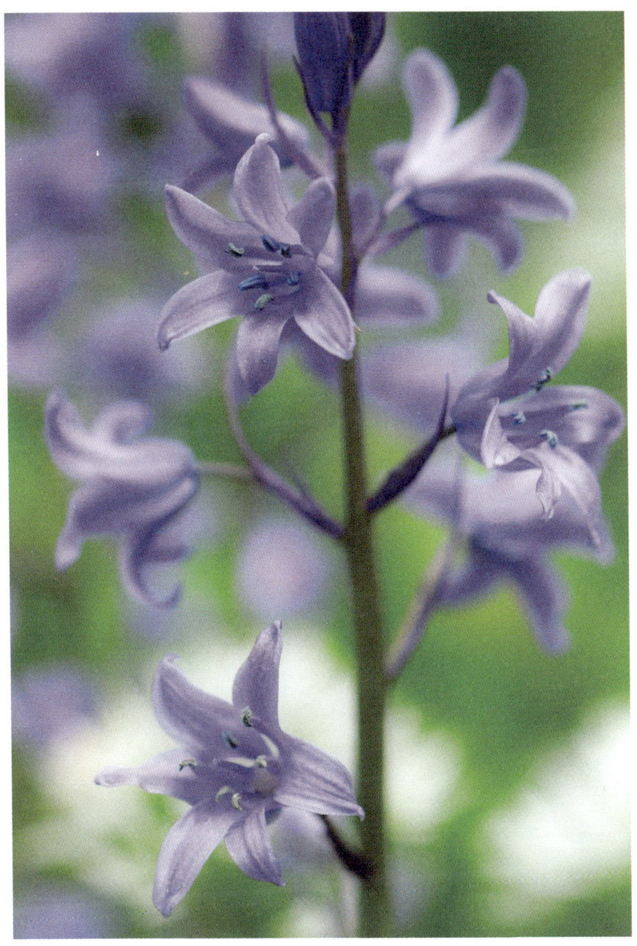

▲ *Posting seasonal images as you shoot will help to keep your stream feel fresh and relevant.*

MACRO NOTES

Consistency is the key to building a following. A strong theme running through your photos will be more appealing to potential followers than a haphazard collection of images. If the theme of your account is macro, don't post pictures of family there too, unless you have a very good and relevant reason to do so.

INDEX

A
abstract images 32–33
analogous color harmony 82, 83
artificial lighting 13
Auto-ISO 8

B
backlighting 28–29
banknotes 74–75
barn doors 80
battery life 45
beaches 16–17, 51
bellows 122–123
black and white images 38, 93, 104–105
blemishes 33
bokeh 40–41
bubbles 100–103

C
camera shake 121
cellphones 10–11
close-up filters 14–15
coastal locations 16–17, 51
coins 74–75
cold weather 44–45
color
    analogous color harmony 82, 83
    complementary 79
    limiting range 82–83
    rainbow images 34–35
    temperature 83, 92–93
    visual weight 31
color checkers 99
color temperature 83, 92–93
commercial product photography 98–99
computer equipment, as subject 84–85
contrast, visual 78–79, 92–93
copy stands 75
cropping images 90, 91
cross-polarization 34–35

D
diffusers 42, 67

E
editing apps 10
electronic equipment, as subject 84–85
extension tubes 22–23
eyes 61, 94–95

F
flames 46–49
flare 38
flash
    diffusion 67, 70
    exposure 67
    lower power settings 109
    off-camera 46
    sync speed 57
    triggering 71
flashlights 58–59
flatbed scanners 54–55
Flickr 124
flowers 26–27, 61, 62–63
focus breathing 118
focus peaking 27, 117
focus stacking 116–119
fossils 50–53
frost-covered objects 44–45
frozen flowers 62–63
fungi 68–69

G
glass, reflections from 36

H
hard light 38–39
High Dynamic Range (HDR) mode 11
high-key images 64–65

I
image editing apps 10
insects 60–61
Instagram 124

J
jewelry 70–71
juxtaposition 78–79, 92–93

K
kitchen utensils 106–107

L
LCD/EVF frame guidelines 88
light sources
    colored 29
    lightboxes 96, 97
    multiple 92–93
    point light 38, 40, 41, 58, 70

light tents 42
light trails 58–59
lightboxes 96, 97
low-key images 80–81

M
M42 lenses 123
magnification figures 19
magnifying glasses 8–9
match flames 46–49
minimalistic images 30–31
minimum focusing distance 37
mirrors 68, 69
money 74–75
Monochrome Picture Style 105
movement, freezing 108
movies 86–87
museums 36–37
musical instruments 120–121

N
negative space 31
Neutral Density (ND) filters 87

O
off-camera flash 46
oil and water images 56–57
optical resolution 55
out-of-focus areas, quality of 40–41

P
panoramic images 88–91
plastic objects 34–35
point light sources 38, 40, 41, 58, 70
polarizing filters 17
product photography 98–99

R
rainbow color images 34–35
red eye 95
reflectors 24–25
repro stands 75
reversing rings 18–19
ring lights 72–73

S
scale 50
scanner photography 54–55
shaded light 21

side-lighting
    and reflectors 25
    and texture 12, 13
Silhouette, Étienne de 29
silhouettes 28–29
simplicity, in composition 30–31
smoke 76–77
snoots 77
soap bubbles 100–103
social media 124–125
soft light 20–21
softboxes 66–67
specular highlights 106
split-toning 93
spot meters 101
stacking 116–119
step-up/step-down rings 15
stereoscopic images 112–115
stitched panoramic images 91
storytelling 42–43

T
texture 12–13
three-dimensional images 112–115
translucency 96–97
TTL (Through The Lens) 67

V
videos 86–87
visual contrast 78–79, 92–93
visual stories 42–43
visual weight 31

W
water droplets 108–111

First published 2022 by
Ammonite Press
an imprint of Guild of Master Craftsman Publications Ltd
Castle Place, 166 High Street, Lewes, East Sussex, BN7 1XU,
United Kingdom
www.ammonitepress.com

ISBN 978 1 78145 462 6

Publisher: Jonathan Bailey
Production Director: Jim Bulley
Design Manager: Robin Shields
Designer: Rhiann Bull
Senior Project Editor: Tom Kitch

Color reproduction by GMC Reprographics
Printed and bound in China

The author and publisher would like to thank the following for the use of copyright material
(hosted by Unsplash): Boris Smokrovic (page 61, top), Z S (63), Damir Omerovi (69), Andres
Vera (71), Guillermo Diaz (93), Umesh Soni (95), Pat Taylor (99), Lanju Fotografie (101 and
102), Hue12 Photography (107), Trac Vu (109), Johnny Brown (110), and Johanna Vogt (121).
All other photographs are © David Taylor, 2022.

How was the book?
Please post your
feedback and photos:
#52AssignmentsMacro

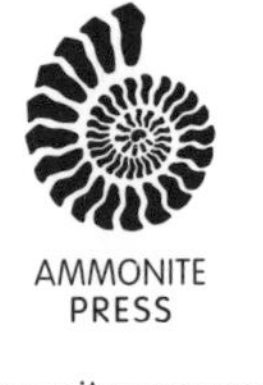

AMMONITE
PRESS

ammonitepress.com

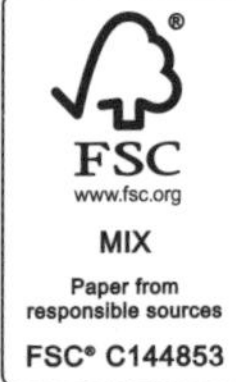